Digital Citizenship
in Schools

Second Edition

Mike Ribble

International Society for Technology in Education
EUGENE, OREGON • WASHINGTON, DC

Digital Citizenship in Schools
Second Edition

Mike Ribble

© 2011 International Society for Technology in Education

Director of Book Publishing: *Courtney Burkholder*
Acquisitions Editor: *Jeff V. Bolkan*
Production Editors: *Tina Wells, Lynda Gansel*
Production Coordinator: *Rachel Williams*
Graphic Designer: *Signe Landin*
Copy Editor: *Cecelia Hagen*
Proofreader: *Katherine Gries*
Indexer: *Potomac Indexing*
Cover Design: *Signe Landin*
Book Design: *Kim McGovern, Barbara B. Gleason*
Book Production: *Barbara B. Gleason*

Library of Congress Cataloging-in-Publication Data
Ribble, Mike.
Digital citizenship in schools /Mike Ribble. — 2nd ed.
    p. cm.
Includes index.
ISBN 978-1-56484-301-2 (pbk.)
1. Education, Elementary—United States—Data processing. 2. Education, Secondary—United States—Data processing. 3. Computer literacy—Study and teaching—United States 4. Internet literacy. I. Title.
LB1028.43.R52 2011
372.34'044—dc23

2011016542

Second Edition
ISBN: 978-1-56484-301-2
Printed in the United States of America

ISTE® is a registered trademark of the International Society for Technology in Education.

SUSTAINABLE FORESTRY INITIATIVE
Label applies to the text stock
Certified Fiber Sourcing
www.sfiprogram.org

About ISTE

The International Society for Technology in Education (ISTE) is the trusted source for professional development, knowledge generation, advocacy, and leadership for innovation. ISTE is the premier membership association for educators and education leaders engaged in improving teaching and learning by advancing the effective use of technology in PK–12 and teacher education.

Home of the National Educational Technology Standards (NETS) and ISTE's annual conference and exposition (formerly known as NECC), ISTE represents more than 100,000 professionals worldwide. We support our members with information, networking opportunities, and guidance as they face the challenge of transforming education. To find out more about these and other ISTE initiatives, visit our website at www.iste.org.

As part of our mission, ISTE Book Publishing works with experienced educators to develop and produce practical resources for classroom teachers, teacher educators, and technology leaders. Every manuscript we select for publication is carefully peer-reviewed and professionally edited. We value your feedback on this book and other ISTE products. Email us at books@iste.org.

International Society for Technology in Education
Washington, DC, Office:
　　　1710 Rhode Island Ave. NW, Suite 900, Washington, DC 20036-3132
Eugene, Oregon, Office:
　　　180 West 8th Ave., Suite 300, Eugene, OR 97401-2916
Order Desk: 1.800.336.5191
Order Fax: 1.541.302.3778
Customer Service: orders@iste.org
Book Publishing: books@iste.org
Book Sales and Marketing: booksmarketing@iste.org
Web: www.iste.org

About the Author

Mike Ribble has worked at several different levels of education. He has served as a classroom biology teacher, a secondary school administrator, a network manager for a community college, and a university instructor. He earned a doctorate in educational leadership from Kansas State University. His interests include technology leadership, professional development, and working with teachers to help enhance teaching and learning with technology. He has written several articles and has presented at national and international conferences and districts on digital citizenship and its effect on the changes within education. Mike is currently a director of technology for a school district in Kansas.

Acknowledgments

I want to thank my family who has always been there to support me.
> To my wife who has always been willing to read my work
> (even after a long day of teaching).
> To my children who have provided perspective on this topic.
> To my mother, father, and brother who taught me about boundaries.

To all the educators around the world who have made the first edition such a success (warranting this updated version).

And to Dr. Gerald Bailey, for all your inspiration and for placing us on the path of becoming better digital citizens.

Contents

INTRODUCTION 1

What's New in This Edition 3

How to Use This Book 3

Who Should Read This Book 6

Additional Resources 6

Section I: Understanding Digital Citizenship 7

CHAPTER 1: The Basics of Digital Citizenship 9

Definition of the Nine Elements 10

Purpose of the Nine Elements 12

Technology in Schools Today—Are AUPs Adequate? 12

The New Citizenship 13

CHAPTER 2: The Nine Elements of Digital Citizenship 15

A Flexible Framework 15

    ELEMENT 1 Digital Access 16

    ELEMENT 2 Digital Commerce 20

    ELEMENT 3 Digital Communication 23

    ELEMENT 4 Digital Literacy 26

    ELEMENT 5 Digital Etiquette 29

    ELEMENT 6 Digital Law 31

    ELEMENT 7 Digital Rights and Responsibilities 35

    ELEMENT 8 Digital Health and Wellness 38

    ELEMENT 9 Digital Security 40

Understanding the Elements 43

Section II: Digital Citizenship in Schools 45

CHAPTER 3: Creating a Digital Citizenship Program 47

Developing a Plan for Digital Citizenship 48

The Digital Citizenship Audit 50

Implementing a Plan for Digital Citizenship 52

Lessons Learned—Ideas from Other Schools or Districts 53

CHAPTER 4: Professional Development Activities
in Digital Citizenship 55

Activity Format 56

Introduction to Digital Citizenship 57

    ACTIVITY 1 Email Bingo (General Digital Citizenship) 57

Learning and Student Performance 60

    ACTIVITY 2 Understanding Digital Technologies (Literacy) 60

ACTIVITY 3   Appreciation Blog (Communication) 61

ACTIVITY 4   New Digital Communication Models (Literacy) 63

ACTIVITY 5   Twitter for Gathering Information (Literacy) 65

ACTIVITY 6   Blogs and Wikis for Parent Communication
(Communication) 67

ACTIVITY 7   Use of Technology in Education (Literacy) 69

ACTIVITY 8   Providing Digital Access Outside School (Access) 70

School Environment and Student Behavior 71

ACTIVITY 9   Appropriate Technology Use (Rights and Responsibilities) 71

ACTIVITY 10 Inappropriate Technology Use (Rights and Responsibilities) 72

ACTIVITY 11 Digital Etiquette Issues (Etiquette) 73

ACTIVITY 12 Digital Citizenship and the District AUP
(Rights and Responsibilities) 74

ACTIVITY 13 Protecting Personal Security (Security) 77

Student Life Outside the School Environment 78

ACTIVITY 14 Digital Rights Management (Law) 78

ACTIVITY 15 Buying Items Online (Commerce) 79

ACTIVITY 16 Technology Addiction (Health and Wellness) 80

Section III: Digital Citizenship in the Classroom 81

CHAPTER 5: Teaching Digital Citizenship to Students 83

Stage 1: Awareness 85

Stage 2: Guided Practice 85

Stage 3: Modeling and Demonstration 86

Stage 4: Feedback and Analysis 86

Incorporating Digital Citizenship into the Curriculum 87

CHAPTER 6: Foundational Lessons in Digital Citizenship 89

Lesson Format 90

FOUNDATIONAL LESSON 1   Appropriate Use or Inappropriate Use? 91

FOUNDATIONAL LESSON 2   Digital Compass 95

FOUNDATIONAL LESSON 3   Recognizing the Nine Elements
of Digital Citizenship 99

FOUNDATIONAL LESSON 4   Digital Driver's License 102

FOUNDATIONAL LESSON 5   What Does It Mean to Be a Digital Citizen? 112

Scoring Rubric for Foundational Lessons 113

CHAPTER 7: Guided Lessons in Digital Citizenship 115

Lesson Format 116

Student Learning and Performance 117

GUIDED LESSON 1   Cell Phone Interruptions (Communication) 117

GUIDED LESSON 2   Message Misinterpretation (Communication) 118

GUIDED LESSON 3   Using the Internet Appropriately (Literacy) 119

GUIDED LESSON 4   How Do Businesses Use Technology? (Literacy)............ 120

GUIDED LESSON 5   MP3 Files for Teaching (Access)................................ 121

GUIDED LESSON 6   Bridging the Digital Divide (Access)........................... 123

School Environment and Student Behavior.. 124

GUIDED LESSON 7   Cyberbullying (Rights and Responsibilities)................... 124

GUIDED LESSON 8   Digital Plagiarism (Rights and Responsibilities)............ 125

GUIDED LESSON 9   Digital Etiquette When Working Online (Etiquette)...... 127

GUIDED LESSON 10   Protecting the School's Network (Security)................... 128

Student Life Outside the School Environment 129

GUIDED LESSON 11   Purchasing Items Online (Commerce) 129

GUIDED LESSON 12   Buying and Selling on Auction Sites (Commerce).......... 130

GUIDED LESSON 13   How Do You Spend Your Free Time?
(Health and Wellness)... 131

GUIDED LESSON 14   Computer Ergonomics (Health and Wellness)............... 132

GUIDED LESSON 15   File Sharing (Law).. 133

Scoring Rubric for Guided Lessons 134

CONCLUSION.. **137**

Digital Citizenship and Parents.. 138

Digital Citizenship and the Law 139

Digital Citizenship and Business.. 139

The Future Is Now 140

Lessons Learned Since the First Edition.. 140

Appendixes

APPENDIX A: Definition of Terms... **143**

APPENDIX B: Bibliography.. **151**

References 151

Further Reading.. 154

APPENDIX C: NETS for Students, Teachers, and Administrators.......... **155**

National Educational Technology Standards for Students (NETS•S)................ 155

National Educational Technology Standards for Teachers (NETS•T) 157

National Educational Technology Standards for Administrators (NETS•A) 159

INDEX.. **161**

Introduction

When talking to people who use technology on a regular basis, does it sometimes seem that they are speaking a different language? Do they talk about texting, Facebook, and Twitter? Do their discussions of "friending," smartphones, and phishing confound and confuse? In 2001, an influential article by Mark Prensky identified two distinctive groups of technology users: "digital natives" and "digital immigrants." Digital natives are identified as young people who have grown up around digital technologies and seem to instinctively understand the technology. Digital immigrants (those new to technology), on the other hand, may be fascinated by and may have adopted many aspects of the new technologies, but because they have not grown up with these digital tools, they don't seem to use them as instinctively as the natives.

Students have grown up in a society surrounded by digital technology. As a result, many teachers see their students as digital natives who already know everything there is to know about technology. Additionally, some teachers do not feel competent as digital immigrants. But the truth is, not all students are as technologically savvy as teachers might assume, and not all teachers are as incompetent as they fear.

Even when students are comfortable using technology, they may not be using it appropriately. Likewise, educators of all skill levels may not understand how to use digital technology effectively. Both students and teachers need to find a common ground. They all need to become members of a digital citizenry.

Over the years, users of technology have come together to interact with one another, creating, in effect, a digital society. This digital society has forged new opportunities for education, employment, and social interaction. A typical society would offer such advantages but also require that its citizens act in a certain way—with the rights of citizenship come responsibilities. Laws are made and consequences are established for not following those laws. However, although a multitude of people do work, play, and learn through digital technology, many individuals still don't know how to be responsible citizens in this digital society.

What are the appropriate behaviors in a digital society? How can an individual learn what is appropriate and what isn't? These are core questions, and this book is an attempt to address them through a "teaching solution" called digital citizenship.

Through this teaching solution, information technology leaders can set the tone for technology use in their schools and districts. Teachers and administrators—the so-called digital immigrants—can learn the norms of digital society. Parents can be provided information on the appropriate use of technology at school and in their homes. Together, these groups can then help the children of this digital age to become principled digital citizens of character and integrity.

But more than a teaching solution, digital citizenship is a way of life. Everyone—digital immigrants and natives alike—needs to understand the digital technology we currently use and prepare for what might be used in the future. Teachers, parents, and students need to explore the frontiers while respecting the limits of these technologies, and recognize the possible effects on themselves as well as on others. And then, after these technologies are understood, users need to evaluate how they have used them. Students can be expected to make mistakes when using technology, but through modeling and direction students need not make the same mistake twice. To reach this outcome, the focus of technology education should not just be on the programs or on the technology itself, but also on the appropriate use of the technology. That is to say, technology education should promote digital citizenship.

Through this discussion of digital citizenship, all users of technology—natives and immigrants—can learn the fundamentals of acceptable use. This book offers a framework for asking what we should be doing with respect to technology. The goal of digital citizenship is to provide a consistent message to students and education professionals so that they can become productive and responsible users of digital technologies.

What's New in This Edition

In the few years since the first edition of *Digital Citizenship in Schools*, technology dependence in education has grown exponentially. Not only has the amount of technology changed, but the tools have changed as well. With the addition of smartphones the options have grown for all users. Social networking has also changed how and how much people communicate with each other. School administrators are rethinking the policy of simply blocking information; instead, they are looking for ways to use new technologies to educate students. This second edition begins to look at these changes and find ways to balance technology and appropriate use.

Also since the publication of the first edition, ISTE's National Educational Technology Standards (NETS) have been refreshed and my original co-author, Gerald Bailey, has retired from his work as professor at Kansas State University and from co-authorship of *Digital Citizenship in Schools*. The professional development activities in Chapter 4, the foundational lessons in Chapter 6, and the guided lessons in Chapter 7 are now correlated to ISTE's *refreshed* NETS for Students, Teachers, and Administrators. All three sets of standards are listed in Appendix C.

The Conclusion of this book includes a Lessons Learned Since the First Edition section that points out several changes in the relationship between education and technology over the past four years. Recent visits to schools and districts all over the world have provided me with some perspective on how different educators are using technology. These changes do not seem to be slowing down. Quite the opposite; there seem to be new technologies and changes in the current tools on an almost daily basis. Some researchers are even seeing mini generation gaps between siblings born only a few years apart (Stone, 2010). All these changes will require educators to keep up with the new and changing skills. With these new digital technologies, digital citizenship is becoming more important than ever.

How to Use This Book

This book is intended as an introduction to digital citizenship and how it can be taught and supported in K–12 schools and districts. Its purpose is to provide a basis for understanding digital citizenship, the current trends in this area, and the potential needs students will face in the future. Written primarily for educators and technology leaders—superintendents, principals, technology coordinators, library media specialists, classroom teachers, and teacher educators—this book is designed to help a district- or site-based team understand digital citizenship and how it can affect their curriculum and schools. Likewise, this book can help individual educators and technology leaders see the importance of digital citizenship and identify ways it can improve teaching and learning with technology.

The goal is not perfection in terms of technology use, but the support of faculty and students in the responsible use of technology. The topic of digital citizenship covers a vast array of technology issues. This book breaks down the various elements and explains them in detail, then offers suggestions on implementing digital citizenship in schools. The discussion is organized into an introduction, seven chapters (contained in three sections), a conclusion, and appendixes.

Introduction

The introduction provides a roadmap for the chapters that follow. It discusses the importance of digital citizenship and tells where to find critical information.

Section I: Understanding Digital Citizenship

Section I is geared toward anyone interested in digital citizenship. The chapters in this section outline the technology issues discussed in the rest of the book. It also provides crucial background information of use to all technology coordinators and teachers.

Chapter 1: The Basics of Digital Citizenship

All technology leaders must have a solid understanding of digital citizenship before making changes to their curriculum. This chapter helps leaders understand the meaning of digital citizenship and what makes it so important.

Chapter 2: The Nine Elements of Digital Citizenship

Digital citizenship is comprised of nine distinct elements. To fully apply the concepts of digital citizenship to a given school or district, technology leaders should review these nine elements to become familiar with digital citizenship in its constituent parts and as a whole.

Section II: Digital Citizenship in Schools

Section II is designed to help technology leaders and administrators determine what they can do to create and support digital citizenship programs in their districts.

Chapter 3: Creating a Digital Citizenship Program

Once technology leaders understand the concepts of digital citizenship, they need a vehicle that allows them to work with the information. The audit in this chapter is designed to help technology leaders determine which elements of digital citizenship need to be addressed most urgently in their schools or districts and which can be dealt with at a later time. This section also provides some ideas and examples of how other districts have implemented digital citizenship.

Chapter 4: Professional Development Activities in Digital Citizenship

Technology coordinators and other educators who use technology need some direction on how best to implement and use digital citizenship in their districts or sites. These activities are designed to help technology leaders educate other technology users in their schools or districts in implementing digital citizenship.

Section III: Digital Citizenship in the Classroom

Section III provides ideas and activities for teachers in the classroom.

Chapter 5: Teaching Digital Citizenship to Students

Chapter 5 helps teachers and library media specialists determine how to effectively incorporate the themes of digital citizenship into the curriculum.

Chapter 6: Foundational Lessons in Digital Citizenship

The lessons in Chapter 6 help teachers and library media specialists raise their students' consciousness of digital citizenship issues.

Chapter 7: Guided Lessons in Digital Citizenship

These activities help classroom teachers work with students to understand the concepts of digital citizenship. Although the lessons here are not as fully articulated as those in Chapter 6, they nonetheless provide resources to begin teaching digital citizenship.

Conclusion

The conclusion summarizes the principles of digital citizenship and addresses topics not covered elsewhere in this book. This section identifies important issues and provides suggestions for how they may be handled as they arise. The section Lessons Learned Since the First Edition focuses on the changes that have occurred since the release of the first edition and on the importance of being prepared to meet those changes.

Appendixes and Index

Refer to Appendix A for terms and definitions relevant to digital citizenship. Appendix B lists the references cited in this book. ISTE's refreshed NETS for Students, Teachers, and Administrators are presented in Appendix C. These standards were refreshed in 2007, 2008, and 2009, respectively. An index is new to this edition.

Who Should Read This Book?

Technology leaders who will benefit from the principles and activities in this book include:

- Teachers and educators

- District planners and administrators

- Lead teachers

- District technology and curriculum coordinators

- Early adopters

- District and site instructional technology specialists

- Professional development personnel

- Site administrators and technical support staff

- Teacher educators

- Library media specialists

Additional Resources

This book highlights a number of resources that teachers may want to reproduce for use in their classroom. Some of these resources may become dated with time. To help keep these resources current, a companion website is available at www.digitalcitizenship.net.

The digitalcitizenship.net website follows the same format as *Digital Citizenship in Schools* and offers materials available for download. As technology changes and additional materials are created, they will be placed on this website. This site will be maintained as long as this book and ISTE's HomePage Book on digital citizenship, *Raising a Digital Child: A Digital Citizenship Handbook for Parents*, are in print.

SCHOOL

HOME

WORK

Section I
Understanding Digital Citizenship

It is a thousand times better to have common sense without education than to have education without common sense.

—ROBERT G. INGERSOLL

What is digital citizenship and why is it important for individuals to become contributing members of a digital society? Moreover, why should anyone—administrators, teachers, parents, students—even be concerned with such a thing as a "digital society"?

The term *citizen* is most commonly defined as "a native or naturalized person who owes allegiance to a larger state or collective and who shares in the rights and responsibilities afforded all members of that collective." As the definition states, a citizen both works for and benefits from a larger society. The concept of digital citizenship, then, reinforces the positive aspects of technology so that everyone can work and play in this digital world.

To date, few social guidelines have been developed for the use of digital technologies. We can decide, as a society, that unacceptable behavior should be the norm. Or we can decide that digital technology should be used for the benefit of all. This is why those who work for and benefit from a larger society need to be involved in deciding how best to support digital technology in our communities. This is why there needs to be digital citizenship.

CHAPTER 1

The Basics of Digital Citizenship

The popular press is increasingly reporting a pattern of misuse and abuse related to technology in our schools, homes, and society in general. This pattern of technology misuse is documented in articles, texts, and countless news broadcasts. Some examples include using text messages or social networking sites to intimidate or threaten students (cyberbullying) (Paulson, 2003), downloading music illegally from the Internet (McGuire, 2004), using blogs or social networking sites such as Facebook to complain about teachers, or using cellular phones to text or play games during class time (Urbina, 2003). Unfortunately, the digital world has come up with few rules about what is and is not appropriate behavior for digital citizens. How individuals behave as members of a digital society (inside and outside school) has become an issue for technology leaders, parents, and society as a whole.

As schools and society become more intertwined with digital technology, there needs to be a structure that can teach students (and parents) how to act with respect to this technology. Very little has been defined in this area. Some stop-gap measures have been created, such as acceptable use policies (AUPs), which are designed to help define the rules of technology use in school. The problem is that few of these AUPs teach the *use* of digital technology. Most often, AUPs simply tell the student what they can and cannot do with technology at school. These rules do not teach students what is appropriate and why, and instead simply define the uses that are *restricted* in the school setting.

ESSENTIAL QUESTIONS

What situations has your school or district experienced in which digital technology was an issue? Were they handled to your satisfaction?

How is your district addressing issues related to digital technology?

This book identifies nine essential elements of digital citizenship to help bring some clarity to these technological situations, not only in our schools but in our society as well. Digital citizenship does not stop at the classroom door. Digital technology has become part of nearly every person's daily life, and it should be our goal that individuals will use technology appropriately in all settings, not just at school. Digital citizenship aims to teach everyone (not just children) what technology users must understand in order to use digital technologies effectively and appropriately. If using technology appropriately is a priority for society as a whole, then teaching students how to use it in this manner should be a priority. By learning about these nine elements of digital citizenship, students can learn to recognize inappropriate technological behavior wherever it occurs.

Definition of the Nine Elements

Digital citizenship can be described as the norms of appropriate, responsible behavior with regard to technology use. I have identified nine elements as a way of understanding the complexity of digital citizenship and the issues of technology use, abuse, and misuse: these nine elements comprise digital citizenship.

As members of a digital society, it is our responsibility to provide all users the opportunity to work, interact, and use technology without interference, destruction, or obstruction by the actions of inappropriate users. Good digital citizens work to help create a society of users who help others learn how to use technology appropriately. Everyone should work together to identify the needs of technology users and provide opportunities to make them more efficient.

The nine elements that serve as the basis for appropriate technology use and form the foundation on which the digital society is based provide a starting place to help all technology users understand the basics of their technology needs. Because there is no way to predict the future, these elements (and possibly others in the future) will help direct users into appropriate usage. By becoming more aware of the issues related to technology, everyone can become better digital citizens and provide opportunities for users to enjoy technology while helping to prevent its misuse and abuse.

ELEMENT 1

DIGITAL ACCESS: full electronic participation in society. Can all users participate in a digital society at acceptable levels if they choose?

ELEMENT 2

DIGITAL COMMERCE: electronic buying and selling of goods. Do users have the knowledge and protection to buy and sell in a digital world?

ELEMENT 3

DIGITAL COMMUNICATION: electronic exchange of information. Do users understand the various digital communication methods and when each is appropriate?

ELEMENT 4

DIGITAL LITERACY: process of teaching and learning about technology and the use of technology. Have users taken the time to learn about digital technologies and do they share that knowledge with others?

ELEMENT 5

DIGITAL ETIQUETTE: electronic standards of conduct or procedure. Do users consider others when using digital technologies?

ELEMENT 6

DIGITAL LAW: electronic responsibility for actions and deeds. Are users aware of laws (rules, policies) that govern the use of digital technologies?

ELEMENT 7

DIGITAL RIGHTS AND RESPONSIBILITIES: those requirements and freedoms extended to everyone in a digital world. Are users ready to protect the rights of others and to defend their own digital rights?

ELEMENT 8

DIGITAL HEALTH AND WELLNESS: physical and psychological well-being in a digital technology world. Do users consider the risks (both physical and psychological) when using digital technologies?

ELEMENT 9

DIGITAL SECURITY (SELF-PROTECTION): electronic precautions to guarantee safety. Do users take the time to protect their information while taking precautions to protect others' data as well?

These nine elements and their core questions form the backbone of Digital Citizenship and the creation of a digital citizenry. All users of technology must act, as well as teach others in appropriate ways. These should be the duties of all digital citizens.

Purpose of the Nine Elements

These nine elements were identified to help educators (as well as all users) better understand the variety of topics that constitute digital citizenship and to provide an organized way to address them. Digital citizenship is not a set of iron-clad rules; rather, it is a way to conceptualize the challenges facing all technology users. The nine elements are a starting point for preparing students to become full-fledged digital citizens. Depending on the situations, some of the elements may be of more concern to technology leaders while others may be more of a focus for teachers.

Technology and the Law

Read more about technology and the law in Lawrence Lessig's 2006 book *Code: And Other Laws of Cyberspace*, Version 2.0. *Code* is published by Basic Books, New York. "Codev2" is also available online: http://codev2.cc/download+remix/.

As new digital technologies emerge, any framework of rules or codified principles will quickly become incomplete and outdated. Rather than attempting to set rules related to technologies, it is better to identify the underlying issue in order to guide users through this ever-changing digital landscape. Lawmakers are creating laws and establishing policies to protect citizens, but they are not enough. These laws and policies fail to focus on the central issue of technology use in a digital society—knowledge. Users need to have a grounded understanding of technology and its appropriate use. In other words, an individual can become a productive and responsible digital citizen only by learning the principles of digital citizenship.

The focus of this book is to begin that discussion. Coming to a consensus on how everyone will cope with digital technology will be difficult, but schools must begin somewhere. Because our schools encompass our future, this is where the discussion should begin.

Technology in Schools Today— Are AUPs Adequate?

Technology leaders or teachers often remark, "We already have an AUP in our district, and it is working fine." However, it is often not enough to simply have an acceptable use policy. We also need to provide active direction to students. Teachers know that the central goal of education is not just reading, science, or math—the central goal is to help students prepare for their future. Technology will be a part of that future. With new and changing technology, users cannot assume that everyone knows what is appropriate and what is not. It is the responsibility of educators and the school community to help define appropriate technology use.

Technology leaders should not assume that, simply because we have a policy in place, the policy is working. When researching articles and statistics from schools using AUPs, evidence has been discovered that these policies are, in fact, not working in critical areas.

Most administrators know that schools need policies that students can follow and teachers can support. Digital citizenship is important for schools because it provides a flexible structure for these policies. A technology team in a district or site can take the nine elements of digital citizenship and define what *their* students need to learn in *their* schools to prepare for the digital future. Moreover, instead of just restricting certain uses of technology, technology leaders can point to the tenets of digital citizenship to show why using technology in a given way is inappropriate.

As the issues change, so must the rules and policies in schools. It is possible to create better AUPs. Better AUPs are easier to enforce:

AUP Resources

Work by Dave Kinnaman, "Critiquing Acceptable Use Policies" (1995–2006), is available to critique AUPs to make sure they are both complete and focused effectively:

> www.prismnet.com/~kinnaman/aupessay

New information on creating acceptable use polices has been collected and organized by the Kentucky Department of Education (2011), Guidelines for Creating Acceptable Use Policies:

> www.education.ky.gov/KDE/Administrative+Resources/Technology/
> Additional+Technology+Resources

> www.education.ky.gov/KDE/Administrative+Resources/Technology/
> Additional+Technology+Resources/Acceptable+Use+Policy+Guidelines+and+State+
> Requirements+for+Student+and+Staff+Access+to+Electronic+I.htm

Kim Fitzer and Jim Peterson write, in Enforcing Acceptable Use Policies (2002), that AUPs are of no utility unless enforced, and the authors give advice on how to minimize potential AUP violations:

> www.ed.uiuc.edu/wp/crime-2002/aup.htm

Bradley Mitchell has written a useful guide on how to create an AUP, available from About.com:

> http://compnetworking.about.com/cs/intranets/ht/ht_createaup.htm

The New Citizenship

It's not an understatement to say that the digital world has changed how people behave and function as citizens of the "real" world. Users live, work and interact not only in the physical world, but in a digital, virtual world as well. Educators must prepare students to live in a world without physical boundaries and help them learn how to work with others, virtual or otherwise. "Citizenship" in this sense takes on a new meaning beyond our normal understanding of geographical nations, states, and communities. Indeed, this new citizenship is global in nature. American children will have to learn how to work with technology users from India, China, Russia and around the world. A common framework, such as digital citizenship, provides everyone with a starting point for understanding each other.

Teaching this new citizenship goes beyond simply expressing rules and polices. All educators must help students understand that digital technology makes them, in a very real sense, citizens of the world. As such, educators should look at technology not just as a collection of toys or gadgets, but as tools that allow individuals to communicate and, ultimately, create society. In short, they need to engage with digital technology in the same way their students already do.

It's not a stretch to say that digital technology has become ingrained in our society, to the point where it is often difficult to separate the technology from the users. Just ask any office worker what he or she would do if the company's computer network went down. The commingling of bits, bytes, headspace, and office space illustrates the importance and challenges of digital citizenship—namely that a balance must be struck between technology and the people who use it.

The next chapter focuses on the nine elements of digital citizenship. By exploring these elements, teachers and technology leaders can gain a better understanding of how the issues of digital technology relate to the concept of digital citizenship.

CHAPTER 2

The Nine Elements of Digital Citizenship

The nine elements of digital citizenship were identified after evaluating hundreds of articles, books, and news broadcasts related to technology use, misuse, and abuse. These nine elements focus on today's issues, though they have the flexibility to accommodate technology changes in the foreseeable future.

A Flexible Framework

The elements provide a framework for understanding the technology issues that are important to educators. They should be used to identify current areas of need in a school or district technology program, as well as emerging issues that may become increasingly important in coming years.

During the research process, I found that although some groups were talking about digital citizenship issues (the Motion Picture Association of America and Junior Achievement have both looked closely at digital copyright, and the University of Pittsburgh has focused on service learning), nowhere could I find was there a systemic review of all the different areas of digital citizenship covered in this book. This is why I believe that this conceptualization of digital citizenship is so important: instead of focusing on a single issue, I address the topic as a whole.

ESSENTIAL QUESTIONS

When reading through the themes, ask yourself these probing questions:

- Which of these issues most need to be addressed in my school or district?

- What issues will my school or district need to address in the next two to four years?

Answers to these questions will help identify which of the elements should be discussed first as areas of need.

In this chapter, each of the nine elements is defined and explained, and then further clarified with examples of appropriate and inappropriate behavior. I offer suggestions on recognizing a given element in the school or classroom and then provide scenarios that reinforce the concepts and behaviors involved.

I've also included some links to websites. These are provided as a place to start your own research; because websites often disappear without notification, because new and often better information gets posted, and because information on a site may not be updated regularly, the information included here may not fit your situation exactly. In addition, I've provided a list of keywords and phrases in each of the elements. Educators need to create a search strategy and use these keywords (as well as others they determine). Doing this will allow for flexibility for the future.

The nine elements provide a lens that technology leaders can use to focus their understanding of digital citizenship issues. Students are already using these technologies; now, school leaders and teachers need to provide them with resources for using them appropriately.

ELEMENT 1

Digital Access

DEFINITION: *Full electronic participation in society*

Technology provides opportunities for large numbers of people to communicate and interact very quickly. However, not everyone has access to all the tools of this new digital society. Because of socioeconomic status, disabilities, and physical location (among other factors), these opportunities are not equally available to all students or teachers.

Groups that are disenfranchised by lack of technology access include families who do not have the financial ability to have technology in the home, school districts that have too few computers for their students (while others have more than enough), and rural schools that lack access to high-speed Internet connections. Educators need to evaluate the use of computers within their schools. Do all students have access throughout the day to technology?

Teachers also need to encourage technology use in their classrooms. In schools where a majority of students do not have access to technology in the home, additional opportunities such as open computer labs, evening access to school libraries, and extracurricular activities should be offered to make up the difference.

Schools and districts need to be aware that some families may not have access to technology on a regular basis. When student information is provided online (e.g., through a parent portal of a student information system or forms on a website), be aware that not all will be able to access the information. When moving to online opportunities, (e.g., student enrollment online) other options such as kiosks, community centers, or open labs may be necessary.

ESSENTIAL QUESTIONS

Does everyone in your school have equal opportunities as far as technology use is concerned?

Do all students have the opportunity to be involved in a digital society?

There are other groups, such as special needs students, who might benefit from the use of technology but who do not have adequate access to the special tools designed for their use. Special needs students require special equipment to make the technology more accessible to them, and districts rarely have an adequate budget to acquire them. Schools and districts should ask themselves, "Are we preparing our students for a future with technology?" If this is a priority (and it should be), then planning for greater access for all students is a necessity.

Schools have been purchasing technology for years, but many schools still have inadequate resources. Even students who enjoy high-quality access at school may not be technologically literate enough to prepare for a future work world filled with technology. A study by the U.S. Department of Education in 2002 showed that only 41% of African American and Hispanic students were using a computer in the home compared with 77% of white students (Mark, 2003). The disparity between those who do and those who do not have access to technology in America is widening, but the issue is not simply a matter of race or socioeconomic status. This is also evident in a 2006 telecommunications report by the U.S. Government Accountability Office (2006), which showed that only 28% of U.S. households had high-speed access, with the rate in rural areas much lower than that of urban neighborhoods because of the need to be within three miles of a central office.

In the recent years the technology trends of minority groups (especially among people of color) have shown marked gains in Internet and broadband adoption. According to the Pew Internet & American Life Project, there has been almost a doubling of Internet use by users who are black or Latino (Smith, 2010b). While the numbers have improved, these groups still lag behind their white counterparts. One area where minorities tend to outpace whites is the ownership and use of cell phones. These groups tend to use many more of the capabilities of cell phones (e.g., text messaging, social networking sites, and the Internet) than do whites (Smith, 2010a). As the trend begins to move more and more to mobile devices, there is a new opportunity for access by individuals and groups. Access will be an issue that will most likely need to be addressed in the very near future, and schools will need to decide whether and how they should become part of this equalization process.

Teachers and administrators need to understand that technology will be important to the future of all students, not just a chosen few. By being more aware of these access issues, schools can explore and advocate for meaningful initiatives such as one-to-one computing (in which all students are given access to a computer) or BYOD—"bring your own device" (where students can bring their devices from home to use in the classroom). Some communities have even gone so far as to provide wireless connections for all members of the community.

Digital Access Issues

- Equitable access for all students

- Accommodations for students with special needs

- Programs for increasing access outside schools

Examples of Inappropriate Digital Access

- Schools ignore or overlook the digital needs of disenfranchised groups (e.g., not viewed as important).

- Teachers fail to accommodate students who do not have access to technology.

Examples of Appropriate Digital Access

- District administrators work toward providing technology opportunities for all students within their schools.

- Technology leaders provide technology to students for use in school and out, such as a one-to-one laptop program.

Digital Access Keywords

- digital divide

- technology and the disabled

- technology access

- technology and minority groups

- digital dirt road divide

Digital Access Scenario

Urban School District's technology coordinator, Mr. Jones, and the school superintendent, Mr. Smith, want to streamline their information gathering efforts. They would like to have parents complete all school forms online.

Inappropriate. Mr. Jones and Mr. Smith send the new policy out to all parents, notifying them that paper forms will no longer be used. They explain that paper copies will not be distributed because the required forms are readily accessed on the school district's website. A number of parents bitterly complain because they do not have regular access to computers. Mr. Jones and Mr. Smith are puzzled because it seems to make the process easier and faster.

Appropriate. Mr. Jones and Mr. Smith discuss requiring parents to complete information online. They conduct a survey to determine how many parents have computer access at home. When reviewing the results, it is clear that students belonging to some minority groups have fewer opportunities to access these resources than other groups. Mr. Jones and Mr. Smith conclude that keeping forms on the school district website is a positive step forward, but that they should keep both options—electronic and paper. They begin to strategize about ways to make technology available to all groups in their school district.

What could make a difference. When using technology, leaders should think about their student population. Some schools may have a large population of technology users, while others may not. They should not forget to consult parents and other community members before requiring that something be done exclusively online.

Web Resources for Digital Access

Public Broadcasting Report on the Digital Divide (archive):
www.pbs.org/teachers/learning.now/digital_divide/

UCLA's The Digital Divide: A Resource List:
www.gseis.ucla.edu/faculty/chu/digdiv/

U.S. Department of Education Reports on the Digital Divide:
www2.ed.gov/Technology/digdiv.html

ELEMENT 2

Digital Commerce

DEFINITION: *The electronic buying and selling of goods*

Digital commerce is often the most difficult element of digital citizenship for educators to address in the classroom. Teachers may believe it is not their responsibility to teach students to be informed, careful consumers (except in certain business courses). However, online purchasing has become an important factor in students' lives. According to Harris Interactive, in 2009 America's youth ages 8–24 (Generation Y) spent $220 billion online. Digital commerce plays a large role in students' lives, so they need to understand all aspects of these online transactions.

Learning to become an intelligent consumer is an important aspect of good citizenship. Unfortunately, it is not uncommon for students to go online and purchase items without thinking about the consequences. Often, the consequences extend beyond accumulation of debt. For example, not knowing how and where to buy items online can leave kids vulnerable to Internet scams and identity theft. If teachers hope to prepare students for the rest of their lives, digital commerce is an important issue that needs to be addressed.

ESSENTIAL QUESTIONS

Are students aware of the opportunities as well as the problems associated with purchasing items using digital technology?

Should students be made more aware of how to purchase goods and services through digital formats?

Students use Internet resources to learn about items they want to purchase, and (increasingly) to buy those items directly online. This practice has been steadily increasing over the last decade. In the Pew Internet & American Life Project report Social Media and Young Adults, nearly half (48%) of online teens purchase books, clothing, or music online (Lenhart, Purcell, Smith, & Zickuhr, 2010). Even with the increase of online purchasing, all Internet users need to learn to be discerning online customers. Many are unsure about how to shop for the best deal, and many more do not know about the hazards of providing sensitive information (such as credit card numbers, bank numbers, or other personal data) to insecure sites. Because using online tools, mobile technology, and social networking to purchase items is rapidly becoming the norm, students should be taught to understand this process.

Digital commerce may not seem to be a particularly important issue for teachers and technology leaders, but it is keenly important for their students. One of the goals of education is to create educated members of a society, thus this is an important skill. Anyone who is actively working, playing, or purchasing items online is a member not only of a digital community but of an economic community as well.

Students need to understand that their actions online can follow them throughout their life (e.g., ruining their credit by running up large credit card debt). If teachers are to help prepare their students to be good citizens, they need to prepare them for interacting in a digital economy.

Digital Commerce Issues

- Online buying through commercial sites, auction sites, and other Internet locations
- Online selling through auction sites and other Internet locations
- Media subscriptions and purchases made through media software such as iTunes
- Buying and selling "virtual merchandise" for online games

Examples of Inappropriate Digital Commerce

- Students purchase goods online without knowing how to protect their identity (leaving them open to identity theft).
- Students fail to realize that poor online purchasing practices lead to poor credit ratings.

Examples of Appropriate Digital Commerce

- Students become informed consumers so they can safely purchase items online.
- Students spend the time to research what they want to purchase, then take the time to identify "safe" sites with the best prices.

Digital Commerce Keywords

- online shopping
- online auction policies
- technology and identity theft
- technology and credit issues

Digital Commerce Scenario

Liz is using the Internet to buy decorations for the homecoming dance. She is unsure of what exactly she is looking for, but wants something that looks nice. She has a limited budget, and she is not really sure what quality decorations might cost.

Inappropriate. Liz finds many decoration options when searching the Internet but none are in her price range. Finally, she finds a website where many of the decorations are 50% less than what she has found on other websites. She immediately puts in an order without researching the company or determining whether her information is secure on that website.

Appropriate. Liz discusses online shopping with her friends and teachers before making a purchase online. They advise her to spend some time researching online merchants and making sure they are secure and legitimate before buying anything from them. She finds a website where the decorations are 50% less than what she sees at other websites. After some research, however, she realizes that this website does not belong to a reputable company. More important, they do not have a secure website for payments. She finds some decorations that are a little more expensive from another company's website. They have a good reputation, with high ratings from previous users. Liz completes her purchase without any complications.

What could make a difference. By interacting with others and discussing the appropriate way to shop online, this student can find what she is looking for and buy it from a reputable dealer. Too often, users just stop at the first site that looks like it will fulfill their needs. To protect against identity theft, users also need to be aware of who can see their information online.

Web Resources for Digital Commerce

Surfing the Net with Kids:
  www.surfnetkids.com/go/safety/186/safe-online-purchasing-practices/

Get Safe Online:
  www.getsafeonline.org/nqcontent.cfm?a_id=1121

ELEMENT 3

Digital Communication

DEFINITION: *The electronic exchange of information*

Cell phones, social networking, and texting have changed the way people communicate. These forms of communication have created a new social structure governing how, when, and with whom people interact.

Digital communication provides users with instant access to others on an unprecedented level. Many businesses prefer using email over a phone call because email provides a record of the message. But there are consequences to this built-in record-keeping feature. Users forget that even though they may delete a message it is usually stored on a server or is backed up for future review. This means users need to think about what they say when using email. This is the same for many other communication methods like texting and social networking sites: even after the information is deleted it continues to "live on" in cyberspace. Any of these technologies can be used inappropriately. Too often, people send emails, texts, or posts without considering who might see them or how they might be interpreted. It is easy to write the first thing that comes to mind and then send it before considering the long-term consequences. In some situations speaking to someone face-to-face can solve a situation faster than multiple emails or other communication methods.

Cell phones allow for mobile personal communication. Many parents now believe their children must have a cell phone—they want to be able to reach their children at all times (Selingo, 2004). But many teachers and administrators see cell phones at school as a major distraction and catalyst for behavioral problems. This is a significant issue for schools and for society in general. Cell phone technologies provide many advantages and freedoms, but we need to weigh that freedom against the responsibility that comes with it, and carefully consider how we teach that responsibility.

Educators face difficult decisions concerning the use of these digital communication technologies in their schools. Cell phones, texting, and social networking can be seen as inappropriate in schools. But are they? The question is, how do these communication methods fit in an educational setting? What positive outcomes do they enable? What potentially negative effects must be mitigated, and how? With these many communication methods, what kind of "digital footprint" (information provided in cyberspace about someone) is being left behind? If these technologies are banned in schools, what message does that send to our students who have access to these devices outside of school? Sites and districts need to assess the extent of the educational values these communication methods and devices provide. Once technology leadership teams determine those values (if any), they also need to decide how to teach students appropriate use of this technology.

Do I use email, cell phone, texting, and social networking technologies appropriately when communicating with others?

What rules, options, and etiquette do students need to be aware of when using digital communication technologies?

Is there a need to be in contact with other people all the time? Do users understand what is appropriate when communicating with other technology users? These are questions that parents, teachers, and administrators need to work together to answer. These technologies are inherently neither good nor bad—it's only use that makes them so—so there is no universal solution to these questions. Digital citizenship provides the framework to help decision makers in schools, sites, and districts to better understand and address these questions.

Digital Communication Issues

- Email

- Cell phones

- Personal video calls (Skype)

- Instant messaging

- Text messaging

- Blogs

- Wikis

- Social networking

Examples of Inappropriate Digital Communication

- Students text during class time.

- Students use text messaging and email shorthand for class assignments when asked to give complete answers.

- Students use text messaging to cheat on tests.

Examples of Appropriate Digital Communication

- Students and teachers use digital communication devices when they will not interrupt what is going on in the school or classroom.

- Digital communication technologies such as social networking sites are used to support student activities in the classroom, such as sharing ideas or writings with others.

- Teachers use blogs to inform parents of classroom activities.

Digital Communication Keywords

- appropriate email use

- texting issues

- cell phone etiquette

- choosing technology communication models

Digital Communication Scenario

Mrs. Baxter, a language arts teacher, explores new, innovative ways for students to write essays in class. She finds a website that describes how teachers can use blogs to help students post their thoughts and ideas on the web. She decides to set up a blog for her students.

Inappropriate. Mrs. Baxter tells her students to navigate to her blog website and record their ideas. She describes the assignment as diary-like writing. After a couple of days, she finds inappropriate postings (e.g., discussions of boyfriends and girlfriends), but she cannot identify the authors. After a week, she shuts down the blog and decides that blogging was a bad idea.

Appropriate. Mrs. Baxter speaks to her class about the process of blogging. She illustrates examples of suitable comments and emphasizes the importance of appropriate use. After a couple of weeks, the students are responding almost every day, and they are coming to class with more in-depth questions that relate to concepts being discussed in class.

What could make a difference. Teachers need to research the use of technology before using it in their classrooms. Just hearing about something that someone else has used in class does not always mean that it will work. Teachers should check around and ask questions about what the technology can and can't do.

Web Resource for Digital Communication

Additional research can be found on many topic areas related to digital communication at the Pew Internet research site: www.pewInternet.org

ELEMENT 4

Digital Literacy

DEFINITION: *The process of teaching and learning about technology and the use of technology*

One of the most important aspects of technology is understanding how that technology works so that it can be used in the most appropriate manner. Although many agree this is important, it is often overlooked. How many people were "taught" how to use a cell phone while they are in the cellular store or kiosk? This is becoming even more of an issue for education. Technology-infused learning is becoming more commonplace every year and is becoming as transparent as the chalkboard and pencil. However, teaching how to use technology appropriately has not kept pace. Learning with technology does not always include instruction on appropriate and inappropriate use. Too often, the focus is on learning the technology itself, with little time given to discussing what is or isn't appropriate.

ESSENTIAL QUESTIONS

Is enough time devoted to learning how to use the technology tools in the classroom?

How can students use digital technologies to take best advantage of the educational opportunities available to them?

Schools have more technology than ever before. According to Duncan's (2010) National Educational Technology Plan, the tools needed by students are moving beyond the computer, laptop, netbook, or smartphone to the cloud. As these technologies move away from the tools we have known, it will become even more important for users to understand how laptops, smartphones, and tablets can be part of their school's curriculum.

Even when digital technologies are readily available, too often teachers have not had adequate professional development on how to use the technology. As a result, teachers have few ideas or plans on what they could do with it in their classrooms (beyond typing papers or doing Internet searches). Teachers need time to learn how to use technology to stimulate student learning. Teachers and districts need to become partners in providing appropriate technology resources. The school's and the district's information technology staffs need to work together to identify appropriate tools for the classroom. What's more, many educators continue to use outmoded concepts and practices in teaching students. In response, students are leaving traditional educational institutions and choosing more innovative ways to learn, which include online learning. Some districts with large numbers of students leaving have been forced to implement their own distance education programs.

With new technologies at their fingertips, students are asking for new ways to learn. Educators should be encouraged to look at alternative ways of presenting information that can engage these students. Schools and districts have the opportunity to create a new age of education and the time begins now.

Digital Literacy Issues

- Learning the digital basics: browsers, search engines, download engines, and email

- Evaluating online resources (determining the accuracy of content on websites and wikis, assessing the trustworthiness and security of online vendors, recognizing phishing attacks, and so on)

- Exploring and developing online learning modes and distance education

Examples of Inappropriate Digital Literacy

- Students choose alternative educational opportunities because their school or district does not offer online classes or a distance education program.

- Teachers do not provide resources and materials that students can get from digital sources (e.g., blogs, websites, podcasts).

Examples of Appropriate Digital Literacy

- Students take online courses (or mixed delivery—part face-to-face, part online) that are designed to keep them interested in the material.

- Teachers use digital technologies in new and innovative ways, such as creating content for the web that can be accessed by students away from the classroom.

Digital Literacy Keywords

- technology education

- online education

- learning computer hardware/learning software

- understanding technology

Digital Literacy Scenario

John is a sophomore at North High School. John is not interested in sitting in a classroom all day to hear boring lectures about information that he does not care about. He enjoys working on his computer at home doing creative projects such as digital animation.

Inappropriate. John decides to drop out of high school and just spend his time creating animation on a freelance basis. After awhile he gets tired of looking for freelance work and tries to get a job as a computer programmer. John keeps getting rejected, not because of his skills, but because he does not meet the companies' basic educational standards.

Appropriate. John talks to his parents about his disillusionment and frustration in attending school. He and his parents meet with the high school counselor, who tells them about a new online school the district is creating. The counselor tells John that he can work at his own pace from his computer and can finish his class work from home, allowing him to continue creating animation in his free time.

What could make a difference. Students need to understand that certain technology skills are critical when entering the work world—just "liking" technology is not enough. We all need to understand how a given technology works and how to use it appropriately.

Web Resources for Digital Literacy

Center for Digital Education:
www.centerdigitaled.com

Center for Media Literacy:
www.medialit.org

Consortium for School Networking:
www.cosn.org

Mid-continent Research for Education and Learning:
www.mcrel.org/topics/EducationalTechnology

Scenarios for Teaching Internet Ethics:
www.uni.illinois.edu/library/computerlit/scenarios

U.S. Department of Education—Office of Educational Technology:
www2.ed.gov/about/offices/list/os/technology/

ELEMENT 5

Digital Etiquette

DEFINITION: *The electronic standards of conduct or procedure*

Responsible digital behavior makes every user a role model for students. Students watch how others use a technology and assume if others can use it in that manner, so can they. The problem with teaching digital technology is that few rules have been established for the proper use of these devices. The proliferation of new technologies has created a steep learning curve for all users. Some users are more adept and in tune than others, and those who lag behind often do not understand the subtle rules that have emerged among early adopters.

ESSENTIAL QUESTIONS

Are students aware of others when they use technology?

Do students realize how their use of technology affects others?

In the past, it was up to parents and families to teach basic etiquette to their children before they reached school. The problem with the new technologies is that parents have not been informed about what is appropriate and what is not. Very often, parents and students alike are learning these technologies from their peers or by watching others use the technology. School technology teams are in a better position to teach kids appropriate digital etiquette.

This can be a difficult process for both students and their parents. Behavior that may be considered poor digital etiquette by older users may be viewed very differently by students. According to a Cingular Wireless survey on mobile phone etiquette, 39% of users said they would answer a ringing phone while having a face-to-face conversation (Greenspan, 2003). In the past, it was polite to excuse oneself from a conversation before doing something else, but today those rules have been bent almost to the breaking point. And with new uses of the technologies (such as texting and social networking) it makes the process even more difficult.

When students see adults using technologies inappropriately, they assume that this is how they should act. This leads to more inappropriate technology behavior. This cycle must be broken soon, as more technologies are coming along and making this process even more difficult. The new technology tools can be seen on TV and in movies, and their use has become mainstreamed. With the lens of digital citizenship, people can evaluate their own technology use, as well as technology use by others. A good digital citizen seeks out feedback from others to evaluate their use of technology, and then makes personal adjustments based on this feedback.

As members of a digital society, we are asked to do what is best for the larger group. To do this, we must think about how our technology use affects others. Good digital citizens respect others and learn ways to use technology courteously and effectively.

Digital Etiquette Issues

- Using technology in ways that minimize the negative effects on others

- Using technology when it is contextually appropriate

- Respecting others online: not engaging in cyberbullying, flaming, inflammatory language, and so forth

Examples of Inappropriate Digital Etiquette

- Students use cell phones to text in class on topics that are not class-related.

- Students communicate on a social networking site without knowing the rules or responsibilities.

Examples of Appropriate Digital Etiquette

- Students work with their teachers to understand what information can be shared from their cell phones or netbooks and when it is appropriate to do so.

- When communicating in a chat room, users learn the rules of the group before becoming involved in the conversation.

Digital Etiquette Keywords

- technology etiquette

- netiquette

- Acceptable Use Policies (AUP)

Digital Etiquette Scenario

Mr. Sheridan, a high school principal, is expecting an important phone call from the superintendent's office this evening. However, he also expected to attend the school play.

Inappropriate. When entering the auditorium, Mr. Sheridan begins to talk to several parents and forgets about the impending phone call. During the play, his cell phone rings loudly. Parents and students begin looking at Mr. Sheridan as he struggles to answer his phone. Because he is flustered by the call, he begins the conversation before he exits the auditorium.

Appropriate. Knowing he does not want to disturb the performance, Mr. Sheridan puts his cell phone on vibrate. In the middle of the second act, the phone vibrates. Mr. Sheridan quickly leaves the auditorium and conducts the conversation in a private location.

> **What could make a difference.** By training ourselves to think about how technology might affect others, we can start to make better decisions. We also need to give others the permission to provide us with constructive criticism on how we use our own digital technology.

Web and Print Resources for Digital Etiquette

WiseGeek—What is Cell Phone Etiquette?:
www.wisegeek.com/what-is-cell-phone-etiquette.htm

National Science Foundation—Ethics and Computing:
www.nd.edu/~kwb/nsf-ufe/

Phoneybusiness.com—Mobile Etiquette:
http://phoneybusiness.com/etiquette.html

A good collection of essays on the ethics and use of technology is Deborah G. Johnson and Helen Nissenbaum's book, *Computers, Ethics & Social Values*, (2006).

ELEMENT 6

Digital Law

DEFINITION: *The electronic responsibility for actions and deeds*

The Internet has made it easy to post, locate, and download a vast array of materials. Indeed, this ability to share information easily is one of the strengths of the Internet. However, users often do not consider what is appropriate, inappropriate, or even illegal when posting or accessing information on the Internet. Users often remark, "We did not think it was wrong—all we were doing was sharing information." The issues of intellectual property rights and copyright protection are very real, and have very real consequences for violations.

These issues were brought to the forefront when the Recording Industry Association of America (RIAA) fined students and others for downloading music illegally (Wired News, 2003). This action caused some technology users to think twice about what is appropriate and illegal for online file sharing. However, in 2009 a three-year compilation of 16 countries by the International Federation of the Phonographic Industry (IFPI) found that 95% of music files were illegally shared (IFPI, 2009). Ironically, a 2003 survey conducted by Ipsos (a market research company) for Business Software Alliance indicated that two-thirds of college faculty and administrators said it is wrong to download or swap files while less than one-quarter of students felt the same way (CyberAtlas, 2003).

ESSENTIAL QUESTIONS

Are students using technology the way it was intended?

Are students infringing on others' rights by the way they use technology?

Should students using digital technologies be accountable for how they use digital technologies?

The new digital technologies are bringing with them a whole new realm of issues that most likely were not imagined by their creators. Often these issues arise from unforeseen and unintended uses of the new technology. For example, the issue of sexting (the taking and sharing of sexually explicit materials, such as nude or semi-nude pictures) has become huge for teens. If the participant is under the age of 16, this can be considered child pornography even if the sender is a willing participant or has sent a self-portrait. If this material is received by a phone (or other device), the person who owns the device can be criminally charged for just having the material (even if that person didn't want it in the first place). Whoever sends the pictures to others can be arrested for the distribution of child pornography (again, even if underage persons take and send pictures of themselves). Conviction for one of these crimes can ruin someone's reputation permanently, and will require that the person register as a sex offender. Each state and country is different, but many have already passed such laws. Even if the laws in your area do not yet cover sexting as a crime, the recipients (or sender) may be in an area where such laws do apply.

Helpful Tip

The legal aspects of student technology use can be a major concern for school administrators. Technology leaders and teachers need to provide resources to help administrators make good decisions. Likewise, teaching students how to make good choices helps not only the students, but the school administrators. Students need to realize that what they do today may affect them in the future.

There will always be people who do not follow the rules of society and who engage in activities that run counter to the ideals of society as a whole. In this regard, digital society is no different. As such, consequences are being established for those who act as inappropriate digital citizens—users who steal others' information, hack into servers, create and release viruses, and so on. As new laws are being drafted, it is important that digital citizens help to decide how to address these activities as they occur. If members of the digital society do not provide information to help determine these good-citizenship policies, the laws passed by politicians will not reflect a good understanding of digital society.

Laws related to technology use are becoming more of an issue for school districts. Even though issues may occur outside the school walls or not on school computers, the effects may still need to be addressed during the school day. Administrators need to provide teachers and students with resources and guidance on what is legal and illegal.

They also need to determine whether their technology rules and policies are supported legally. Digital citizenship helps all technology users become more aware of the legal ramifications of technology use.

Digital Law Issues

- Using file-sharing sites

- Pirating software

- Subverting Digital Rights Management (DRM) technologies

- Hacking into systems or networks

- Stealing someone's identity

- Sexting and sharing of illicit photos

Examples of Illegal Technology Use

- Students download copyrighted music from social networking or file-sharing sites (e.g., Kazaa).

- Students scripting (using computer code) to bypass firewalls or other network protection.

Examples of Legal Technology Use

- Students understand what can be downloaded without charge and what is considered copyrighted material and should be paid for.

- Students inform an adult of others sharing nude or semi-nude photographs (sexting).

Digital Law Keywords

- technology copyright laws

- Person-to-Person software (P2P)

- software piracy

Digital Law Scenario

Patrick keeps himself very busy. He goes to school, plays on the football team, and has a part time job. Tonight Patrick's boss has asked him to work a little later, and he does not get home until 11 p.m. He realizes that he has a paper due the following morning for his English class. He sits down at his computer and thinks about the time he will need to put into getting a good grade on the paper. He goes to the Internet to do some research and finds the exact information that he needs. All he has to do is copy and paste the information.

Inappropriate. Patrick decides to copy the information from the website and quickly finish the paper. He hands in the paper to his English teacher the next day. The teacher reminds the class that she is using the site TurnItIn.com to check papers for plagiarism. Because Patrick copied the information word for word, he is sure he will be caught.

Appropriate. Patrick decides to work on the paper and cite the source from the website. Because the assignment was rather lengthy, he talks to the teacher before class to explain his situation. The teacher gives Patrick an extra day to finish his paper.

What could make a difference. Teachers must carefully explain to students that, although the Internet is a good source of information, material should not to be taken from it without citing the source. Students need to know that some websites are not as credible as others, and need to be careful of the information they find. Students should look at several sources to confirm the information they find.

Web Resources for Digital Law

The Free Expression Policy Project—Media Literacy: An Alternative to Censorship:
    www.fepproject.org/policyreports/medialiteracy.html

Law Research—Internet Law:
    www.lawresearch.com/practice/ctwww.htm

Ethics in Computing—Technology and Ethics:
    http://ethics.csc.ncsu.edu/basics/

United States Department of Justice—Computer Crime & Intellectual Property Section:
    www.cybercrime.gov

ELEMENT 7

Digital Rights and Responsibilities

DEFINITION: *Those requirements and freedoms extended to everyone in a digital world*

When discussing the membership within a group, people often note that certain rights or privileges come with membership in that group. When someone is given membership rights, there is an assumption that the person will act in accordance with the rules that govern that group. This is true for digital society as well, in which membership allows users to use digital content while enjoying certain protections. In the digital world, users should expect that if they post information to a site (whether it is a poem, a picture, a song, or some other form of original research or creative expression), others will enjoy it without vandalizing it, passing it off as their own, or using it as a pretext to threaten or harass.

ESSENTIAL QUESTIONS

What rights and responsibilities do students have in a digital society?

How do we make students more aware of their rights and responsibilities when using digital technologies?

Being a full member in a digital society means that each user is afforded certain rights, and these rights should be provided equally to all members. Digital citizens also have certain responsibilities to this society; they must agree to live according to the parameters that are mutually agreed upon by members. These boundaries may come in the form of legal rules or regulations, or as acceptable use policies. In a perfect world, those who partake in the digital society would work together to determine an appropriate-use framework acceptable to all. The alternative is to have laws and rules thrust on them.

Helpful Tip

Use scenarios to help draw attention to what is happening in the school and classroom. Encourage students to provide examples of technology use and discuss what might be considered appropriate or inappropriate.

Through the guiding principles of digital citizenship, we offer a means to achieve appropriate behavior in a digital society. This is not just pie-in-the-sky idealism. Some technology companies including Google already adhere to basic good-citizenship tenets, such as "do no harm." If schools are to help form a strong digital citizenry, then such values need to be taught to students, as they will be the next generation of digital technology users. Now is the time to provide a structure for technology use for a digital society. Digital citizenship can help create the framework, but school technology teams will have to come together to determine how their organizations will handle unsociable digital behavior. Students need to be given a clear understanding of the behavior that is required of them to be members of the digital society.

When creating or publishing anything, students should be allowed to protect those works (or not) as they see fit. Digital citizens should have the right of ownership of their work. They should also have the right of free speech in the truest sense: If they wish to make their creations freely available to the entire world, they should be allowed to do so.

Rights and responsibilities are sometimes difficult to define. Users need to understand the difference between what is possible for the individual and what should be done for the good of the group. By adhering to the structure of digital citizenship, the vast majority of users will enjoy the benefits of digital technology because they will understand that there can be rights in a society only if there are also responsibilities.

Digital Rights and Responsibilities Issues

- Following acceptable use policies and using technology responsibly both inside and outside school

- Using online material ethically, including citing sources and requesting permissions

- Using technology to cheat on tests and assignments

- Reporting cyberbullies, threats, and other inappropriate use

Examples of Inappropriate Digital Rights and Responsibilities

- Students use material from the Internet without properly citing the source.

- Students violate their school's AUP because they view it as unfair.

Examples of Appropriate Digital Rights and Responsibilities

- Students cite websites or other digital media sources when using information for class projects.

- Educators inform students of their rights when using digital technologies, but also instruct them on their responsibilities.

Digital Rights and Responsibilities Keywords

- understanding technology rules

- helping others online

Digital Rights and Responsibilities Scenario

Mrs. Jones is the principal of the local high school. Her technology coordinator, Mr. Young, comes to Mrs. Jones and indicates that he sees students accessing pornographic websites. Mr. Young says that he has a demo of an inexpensive web filter that could be used to solve the problem.

Inappropriate. Mrs. Jones agrees that students need to be prevented from accessing these inappropriate sites at school. She tells Mr. Young to purchase the software and put it on the network. A month later, a teacher comes to Mrs. Jones and says that students are unable to access specific research sites on the Internet. The teacher has spoken to the technology coordinator, who says that Mrs. Jones approved the purchase of the software without informing the staff. Several teachers are upset because their students are working on legitimate projects, but access to critical sites is being blocked.

Appropriate. Mrs. Jones asks the technology coordinator to gather information about this web filter as well as other options that could be implemented. She indicates that this information will be brought to the school's technology committee for discussion and approval. Mrs. Jones puts this issue on the next month's agenda for discussion. At the meeting, the technology committee recommends the software purchase as well as staff development for everyone who will be affected by the web filter.

What could make a difference. School administrators, technology committee members, and faculty need to work together to educate students effectively on digital rights and responsibilities. By discussing the issues, all sides can understand why decisions are made. This approach can also generate new ideas for supporting digital citizenship in the classroom.

Web Resources for Digital Rights and Responsibilities

National Educational Technology Plan:
   www.nationaledtechplan.org

Partnership for 21st Century Skills:
   www.p21.org

Privacy Rights Clearinghouse:
   www.privacyrights.org

ELEMENT 8

Digital Health and Wellness

DEFINITION: *Physical and psychological well-being in a digital technology world*

Students need to be aware of the physical dangers inherent in using digital technology. According to Alan Hedge, director of the Human Factors and Ergonomics Research Group at Cornell University, "… carpal tunnel syndrome isn't the only injury to worry about when working at a computer" (Manjoo, 2003, para. 10). Eyestrain and poor posture are not uncommon in digital technology-related activities.

Too often, technology safety concerns relate only to the security of equipment and not the physical well-being and security of students. Sometimes computers are set on tables that are too high or too low for younger users. Adults should not hope that students will simply adapt to the surroundings, nor should they think that students will stop using a given digital device before it causes problems.

ESSENTIAL QUESTIONS

How can students be physically affected by technology?

Are students aware of the physical dangers that can accompany the use of digital technology?

How else can someone become injured using technology?

In addition to the physical dangers, another aspect of digital safety that is receiving more attention is the topic of "Internet addiction." It's a double-edged problem: Not only do users become dependent on the online experience, but they may also irreparably harm themselves physically. Taken to its extreme, Internet addiction can cause both psychological as well as physical problems. This is an issue that is being recognized around the world. Some addiction experts are finding that the withdrawal symptoms associated with Internet addiction are similar to those of alcoholics.

To prevent various technology-related physical injuries, educators need to encourage students to use technology in a responsible way. Making sure that all computer workstations are ergonomically sound is one way to protect students from long-lasting problems related to technology use. But even beyond the physical aspects, adults need to be aware of the amount and type of technology used by students.

Digital Health and Wellness Issues

- Using proper ergonomics and avoiding repetitive motion injuries

- Becoming addicted to the Internet or to video games and withdrawing from society

Examples of Inappropriate Digital Health and Wellness

- Administrators and teachers ignore the possible harmful physical effects of technology on students.

- Teachers do not model proper ergonomics when using technology.

Examples of Appropriate Digital Health and Wellness

- Technology leaders learn how to promote health and wellness with technology.

- Teachers model digital safety in their classrooms and expect their students to do the same.

Digital Health and Wellness Keywords

- technology addiction

- technology and good health

- computer ergonomics

Digital Heath and Wellness Scenario

Rob, a junior at Anyschool High, has enjoyed using the computer since fifth grade. When he entered high school, his parents purchased a laptop for him. Rob is able to take it to school and use it in his room; he can work on it wherever he wants. Rob uses his computer several hours a day in awkward positions. Lately, he has been noticing pain in his lower arms and wrists. At first, the pain wasn't bad; now, it has become increasingly painful to use his keyboard.

Inappropriate. Rob does not tell his parents because he knows that they will take him to the doctor. He is afraid the doctor may want him to decrease the amount of time he spends on the computer and will tell his mom to restrict his computer privileges.

Appropriate. Rob is concerned about losing computer privileges because he is sure that keyboarding is causing his physical pain. He decides to tell his mother about the pain anyway, and she takes him to the doctor. The doctor indicates that there is some inflammation but no major damage. The doctor teaches Rob a set of exercises to avoid repetitive stress syndrome that he can use while at home or school. Rob models these techniques to his computer teacher. The computer teacher decides to have students in class practice these exercises during class.

What could make a difference. The physical and psychological aspects of using technology should not be overlooked. As students start to use digital technologies at ever-younger ages, parents and teachers need to be aware of health issues that might occur. By keeping these issues in mind, teachers and parents can identify and resolve problems earlier.

Web Resources for Digital Health and Wellness

The Center for Internet Addiction Recovery:
www.netaddiction.com

Computer Ergonomics for Elementary Schools:
www.orosha.org/cergos/

University of Nebraska–Lincoln Engineering Electronics Shop—
Computer Related Repetitive Strain Injury:
http://eeshop.unl.edu/rsi.html

U.S. Department of Labor—Computer Workstations Checklist:
www.osha.gov/SLTC/etools/computerworkstations/checklist.html

ELEMENT 9

Digital Security

DEFINITION: *The electronic precautions to guarantee safety*

As more and more sensitive information is stored electronically, a correspondingly robust strategy should be developed to protect that information. At the very least, students need to learn how to protect electronic data (e.g., using virus protection software, erecting firewalls, and making backups).

The idea of protecting what we have should not be foreign to anyone. We put locks on our doors, mount smoke detectors in our homes, and install security systems designed to protect our families and possessions. As a repository of personal information, a personal computer should have as many (if not more) security features as the home that surrounds it. Why should anyone go to the trouble of installing these additional protections? Because technology intruders do not break in through the front door—they hack in through your Internet connection. Any computer that does not have virus protection (with up-to-date virus definitions) is vulnerable. Any computer connected 24/7 to the Internet without firewall protection is defenseless against a snooper on the prowl. Having a wireless network without encryption is tantamount to offering free access to any and all comers.

ESSENTIAL QUESTIONS

How do students protect their technology in a digital society?

How can students be taught to protect themselves and their equipment from harm?

More often than not, security faults occur not because of flaws in the equipment but because of the ways people use it. We give away our passwords without thinking of the consequences. We do not take the time to speak to our children about the possible dangers of meeting people on the Internet. Young people often view strangers on the

Internet as potential friends they have not yet met (Gross, 2009). Too often, students correlate their social status in the digital world with the number of online "friends" they have linked to their Facebook or MySpace pages.

Many hackers are very good at what they do. Professional-looking *phishing* (using an email or other message to try to get a user to send sensitive information to a hacker) programs ensnare users every day. It is up to users to be diligent in protecting their information.

Protecting one's equipment is not just a personal responsibility—it also helps protect the community. By keeping virus software up-to-date, for example, viruses will not get passed along to infect others as easily. However, digital security goes beyond protecting equipment. It includes protecting ourselves and others from outside influences that might cause harm.

Digital Security Issues

- Protecting hardware and network security

- Protecting personal security: identity theft, phishing, online stalking

- Protecting school security: hackers, viruses

- Protecting community security: terrorist threats

Examples of Inappropriate Digital Security

- Teachers or students fail to maintain current software updates or patches that protect their computers from viruses and exploitation.

- Students fail to protect their identity when using email, social networking, or text messaging.

Examples of Appropriate Digital Security

- Users take the time to make sure their virus protection and firewalls are properly updated and configured to protect personal information.

- Teachers and parents talk to students about the dangers of providing information to anyone over the Internet.

Digital Security Keywords

- technology protection

- spyware/adware

- data backup

- firewall

- technology disaster protection

Digital Security Scenario

Adam's school provides email accounts to all students. Adam is afraid that he might forget his password and writes it down in his notebook. One day during class he is called to the counseling office. He leaves his books in class and goes to the office. When he gets back, he sees his notebook open to the page with his password.

Inappropriate. Not thinking anything about it, Adam gathers his books and goes to his next class. The next day, he is called to the office to see the assistant principal, who informs him that another student has reported receiving a threatening email from his account. The student receiving the email did not know Adam and was not sure why he had sent the email. Adam tells the assistant principal that he did not send the email and that someone else must have his password.

Appropriate. Adam is concerned that his notebook was open to the page with his password. He immediately goes to a computer, logs in, and changes his password. Adam decides that he needs to keep his password in a more secure location.

What could make a difference. Students need to be aware that their password is the key to their digital identity. Students should understand that leaving passwords and other personal information out where others can see them might allow others to use their accounts for inappropriate behavior. Passwords should be kept in secure places or memorized to keep them safe.

Web Resources for Digital Security

Center for Safe and Responsible Internet Use:
http://csriu.org

Educational CyberPlayGround:
www.edu-cyberpg.com/schools

Educator's Guide to Computer Crime and Technology Misuse:
www.uni.uiuc.edu/~dstone/educatorsguide.html

Understanding the Elements

The nine elements of digital citizenship are not simple, stand-alone issues. They relate to each other in a dizzying variety of ways. To help teachers and technology leaders better understand how these different elements interconnect, they have been grouped into three categories based on their immediacy to the typical school environment. These categories combine the elements that:

- directly affect student learning and academic performance,

- affect the overall school environment and student behavior,

- affect student life outside the school environment.

When digital citizenship is framed in this manner, teachers and technology leaders can approach it in a way that can have an immediate effect on their school's or district's use of digital technologies (see Figure 2.1).

So where should schools begin? How do technology leaders and teachers decide what to work on first? The first priority of any digital citizenship program will depend entirely on what is currently in place in the district or school. If a school has issues with basic knowledge of new technologies (such as texting or social networking) perhaps student learning and academic performance will be a priority. If a school is having issues with cyberbullying, maybe the priority will be on the overall school environment and student behavior. If students are exhibiting physical or psychological problems related to overuse of technology, then perhaps the initial focus of the program should be on student life outside the school environment.

A Closer Look at Technology in Schools

For another model for technology use in schools, see Gerald Bailey's article "Technology Leadership: Ten Essential Buttons for Understanding Technology Integration in the 21st Century" (1996).

Technology leaders should discuss which elements of digital citizenship should receive highest priority in their districts. Elements that appear to be less important today still need to be identified and understood, even if not set as high priorities. New technologies bring problems that educators cannot foresee; for example, when text messaging technology was added to cell phones, educators did not immediately see any problem with it until students began sharing test answers. Technology leaders need to be constantly vigilant to new, emerging uses of technology, and have a thorough understanding of the nine elements of digital citizenship.

Some topics related to digital citizenship are so important that they should be explored and integrated into educational lessons. In Sections II and III of this book, lesson plans and activities are provided that explore each of the nine elements of digital citizenship. These lesson plans and activities are designed to help technology leaders begin their exploration of digital citizenship.

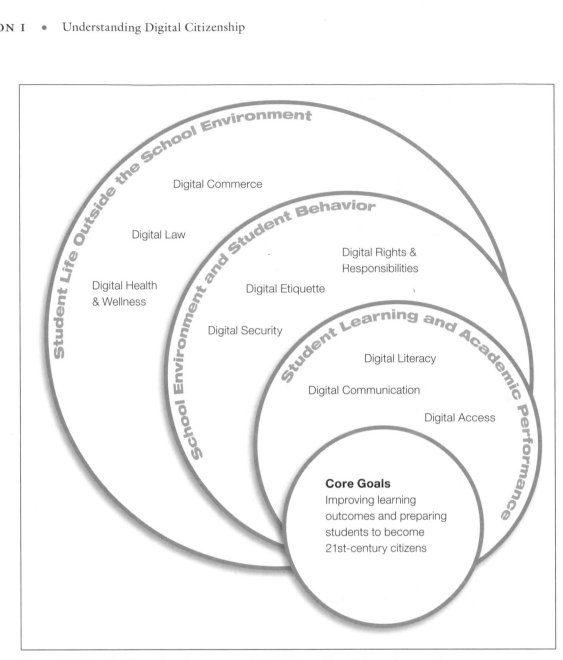

Figure 2.1 Model of how the elements of digital citizenship relate and connect.

Because technology is becoming ever more accessible and students are using these technologies more frequently (both in school and out), technology leaders must continually assess and determine their priorities in terms of digital citizenship. The nine elements of digital citizenship and these three categories should help technology leaders not only relate better to these new technologies and enjoy their benefits, but help all of us realize that there is much we do not know and much we have left to learn.

TEACHERS

ADMINISTRATORS

TECHNOLOGY LEADERS

TECHNOLOGY COORDINATORS

PRESERVICE TEACHERS

Section II
Digital Citizenship in Schools

We live in a society exquisitely dependent on science and technology, in which hardly anyone knows anything about science and technology.

—CARL SAGAN

Placing students, teachers, and administrators on the path to digital citizenship requires the work of many people. One of the key players in this process is the technology leader. The technology leader is the administrator, technology coordinator, or teacher who is responsible for leading the technology work done in the school, site, or district. This section focuses on technology leaders and what they need to do to create a successful digital citizenship program.

Technology leaders will be responsible for educating teachers, administrators, parents, and community stakeholders about the importance of digital citizenship—both inside and outside school. The activities and exercises in Chapter 3 help make everyone more aware of the importance of digital citizenship. Once technology leaders feel comfortable with the concept of digital citizenship they can move to Chapter 4, where lesson ideas for professional development workshops are offered for each of the nine elements.

CHAPTER 3

Creating a Digital Citizenship Program

School technology leaders are in a position to set the tone for appropriate technology use by educating teachers, administrators, parents, and community members about digital citizenship. By employing a teaching model—rather than simply creating policies against technology misuse and abuse—technology leaders can create a self-sustaining digital citizenship program that will benefit all aspects of school technology use. This chapter explores how leaders can initiate this process.

All members of the school community need to be awakened to the importance of digital citizenship and its connection to current policies and future practices. A technology leadership team should be established that brings together representatives from all areas of the school community—administration, faculty, classified staff, parents. This team should begin by identifying the specific needs of the school or district (and the community around them) as they relate to the nine elements of digital citizenship. While every member will come with particular concerns and motivations, the team's common goal should be to establish a program that will enhance the appropriate use of technology for learning, collaboration, and productivity at all levels.

Developing a Plan for Digital Citizenship

Once a technology leadership team is in place, it is important that all members acquire a baseline awareness of digital citizenship issues. The following discussion suggests five steps to begin this process. These steps are depicted graphically in Figure 3.1.

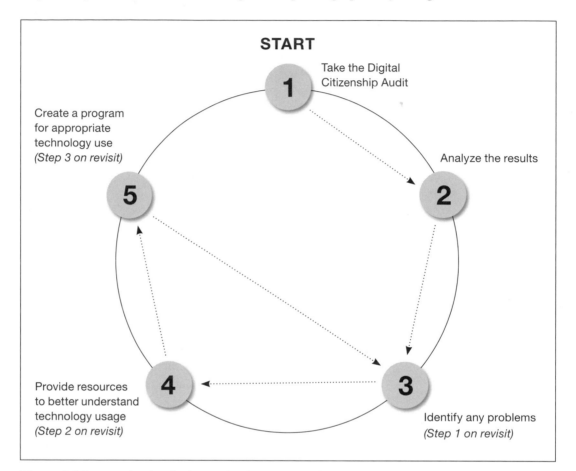

Figure 3.1 Process for developing a plan for digital citizenship.

Step 1. Have members of the technology leadership team complete the Digital Citizenship Audit (see section following these steps). The audit takes only a few minutes and will help determine which elements of digital citizenship are significant issues in your school or district. The Digital Citizenship Audit is a quick way for technology leaders to determine whether technology resources are being properly used, or being misused or abused.

Step 2. Analyze the results of the audit, using the scoring guide.

Step 3. From the results gathered in Step 2, the technology leadership team should ask themselves: Are there significant problems? If so, are the inappropriate technology activities in violation of laws, rules, or policies? Are these activities causing physical or emotional harm to students? Are these activities disrupting the educational process? How aware of these problems are teachers, students, board members, and community members?

If the scores are low (10–19), the team leader should spend some time addressing these issues and informing stakeholders. Look for ways that other schools of similar size and location have addressed these issues.

If the team finds no problems of significance, the team leader should be prepared to share some of the examples and scenarios from Chapter 2 that illustrate the nature of the nine elements of digital citizenship. This will inform the team of possible problems that they may not have considered or that may appear in the near future.

Step 4. Consider the following questions as a team, exploring each member's feelings about the different elements of digital citizenship:

- Should all students have equal access to technology? Unlimited access?

- What issues related to buying and selling items online are appropriate to address in school?

- What should students know about using communication technologies in school? Should limits be placed on those technologies?

- How do students currently use technology to learn new ideas? What might they be able to learn if their technology literacy and access were higher?

- How does student technology behavior affect others in the school community?

- What do students and teachers need to know to keep themselves safe when using technology? Do students understand how to protect their identity when online?

- Do students and teachers know the difference between legal and illegal uses of technology? How do they demonstrate this?

- Do students act responsibly and courteously when using technology?

If any business owners are on the team, have them discuss the importance of appropriate technology use in running their business. If members are still having trouble grasping the many interrelated issues of digital citizenship, the leader should implement some or all of the activities in Chapter 4.

Step 5. Once a consensus is reached on the most important issues and priorities, the leadership team should begin the process of designing a program to teach and model good digital citizenship. The team should focus on these questions as they design the program:

- With regard to technology use, how does our emphasis on "rules and regulations" compare with the schools' emphasis on "education of all stakeholders"?

- Where should digital citizenship be taught in the curriculum? How can room be made for it?

- Who should teach digital citizenship?

- What kinds of staff development opportunities need to be provided first for the program to be effectively implemented?

Once the digital citizenship program is under way, the team should periodically revisit Steps 3–5 to evaluate their progress. The program should be flexible enough to account for changes in technology and usage patterns. As technology changes, so should the digital citizenship program.

Technology has become an integral part of teaching and learning. However, some students are learning and practicing poor digital technology habits. A quality digital citizenship program will require all participants to raise their awareness of how they are using technology, how it affects others, and how inappropriate use can be avoided. Technology leaders must raise their expectations for technology-infused teaching and learning, and focus on the effective and appropriate use of technology for learning. Technology leaders cannot afford to do anything less if they expect to develop productive digital citizens.

The Digital Citizenship Audit

Consider the relative importance and frequency of the activities, behaviors, and concerns related to digital citizenship presented in Table 3.1, and rank each item from 5 (extremely important) to 1 (extremely unimportant). Then use the following scoring guide to interpret your score.

Scoring Guide. Tally your score for each item in the last column to the right, then add them together for a total score.

40–50 This score shows that use of technology is high in this school or district. Unfortunately, inappropriate technology use is also very high.

30–39 Technology use in this school or district is moderate to high. With increased use there is above average technology misuse as well.

20–29 A score in this range denotes the middle of the road. Either the school or district is not using a great deal of technology or educators are unaware of the issues related to digital citizenship.

10–19 A score in this range indicates a low amount of inappropriate technology use. The school or district is either not using technology or the digital citizenship problems are minimal.

This holistic score provides a thumbnail sketch of your needs and engagement with digital citizenship issues. High scores are not entirely bad news. Although a high score indicates that your students may not be following good digital citizenship practices, it also means that you have a high level of technology use in your school.

Table 3.1 Digital Citizenship Audit Form

DIGITAL CITIZENSHIP	Extremely Important	Somewhat Important	Neither Important or Unimportant	Somewhat Unimportant	Extremely Unimportant	Score
Using cell phones to text message test answers to other students	5	4	3	2	1	
Using email or web-sites to intimidate other students	5	4	3	2	1	
Downloading music files illegally from the Internet	5	4	3	2	1	
Being unable to complete class projects or research activities because of a lack of access to technology	5	4	3	2	1	
Using a computer in an awkward position	5	4	3	2	1	
Plagiarizing information obtained from the Internet	5	4	3	2	1	
Using cell phones during class time	5	4	3	2	1	
Posting private information on the Internet	5	4	3	2	1	
Going online to buy and sell items on auction sites during school	5	4	3	2	1	
Dropping out of school for lack of distance learning alternatives	5	4	3	2	1	
					TOTAL SCORE	

These scores have implications both inside educational institutions as well as out in the workplace. As students are trained (or not) in schools, they will take this information (or lack of it) into the workplace with them.

Implementing a Plan for Digital Citizenship

Here are some points that technology leaders need to think about when implementing a digital citizenship plan:

- Make digital citizenship a priority in the district and building technology plan by explaining its importance to students' futures and the future of society as a whole. If schools and districts are to effectively use technology for learning and skills development, digital citizenship must become a key element of that plan.

- Encourage your technology leadership team to look at and discuss the nine elements of digital citizenship from every perspective. Digital citizenship is not a one-time issue. Technology and technology use is always changing, so these issues must be readdressed on an ongoing basis.

- Engage all stakeholders (especially parents) in dialogue on digital citizenship issues, using the essential questions from Chapter 2 as a starting point for discussion. It is not enough to look at this issue from the inside. School leaders should listen to the perspectives and concerns of community members from outside the school environment as well, to gain a greater appreciation of where these issues manifest themselves outside of school.

- Empower the technology leadership team to identify and prioritize the steps needed to address digital citizenship in curriculum, staff development, and board policy. Provide them with a clear understanding of the areas that are of most immediate concern, and identify the skills that will make the biggest difference in the way students use technology to learn and succeed.

- Create a plan to integrate digital citizenship into all curricular areas. Identify ways to reinforce the idea of appropriate use in all technology-related assignments. Digital citizenship issues and skills should not be relegated to the computer lab; instead, they should become an integral part of content learning in all disciplines.

- Educate teachers on the concept of digital citizenship so they feel comfortable speaking on the subject in their classroom. Section III provides ideas and activities for teaching digital citizenship in the classroom. If teachers do not fully understand digital citizenship, they will not be able to help or direct student use of technology in the classroom.

A comprehensive dialogue about digital citizenship is long overdue in most schools and districts. If we hope to create digital citizens who know right from wrong and appropriate from inappropriate behavior in the digital age, technology leaders must make digital citizenship a top priority in their school districts. If not here, where? If not now, when? If not you, who?

Lessons Learned— Ideas from Other Schools or Districts

Since the first edition of this book was published, an increasing number of schools and districts have discussed the topic of digital citizenship, and some have moved rapidly to adopt its elements and principles into their policies and procedures. Here are a few examples of schools and districts that are using digital citizenship to provide resources for their faculty and staff.

Pike County Schools, Pikeville, Kentucky, U.S.

The Pike County Schools have been strong supporters of digital citizenship for several years. One of the projects they began with was a Digital Citizenship Month, during which they covered different elements of digital citizenship each week. During the month they also had contests for students to create ways to inform others about the issues of inappropriate technology use. In their second year, the schools again had digital citizenship activities and, now that their students understood the basics, the high school students acted as mentors for the elementary students, helping them to understand the various topics. Through their community outreach personnel, the schools in Pike County also began talking to parents about the issues of digital citizenship and how the schools could be a partner in this discussion.

Battle River School Division, Alberta, Canada

This school division took a year to rewrite their acceptable use policies, using the nine elements as their foundation. Since they have been using these new AUPs, they have seen a decrease in the number of inappropriate technology activities in their upper-division schools.

International School of Brussels, Brussels, Belgium

The International School of Brussels has been moving toward a 1-to-1 (typically one laptop to one student) initiative with their Grade 7–12 students. They are working on a plan to involve parents in understanding the technology and the issues that go with it by hostng technology nights during which staff talks with parents about the reason for their move to 1-to-1, as well as about ways to help support their students in using the technology appropriately.

Other Examples

There are other examples of schools and districts making their staff and students aware of the issues surrounding technology use. In October 2008, then-President Bush signed an update to the Universal Services Administrative Company's E-Rate program. In this program, schools and districts receive funding for telecommunication services and for some equipment. Schools receiving USAC E-Rate funding are now required to teach their students about Internet safety as well as secure and proper online behavior.

Digital citizenship is helping schools and districts to begin creating the foundation for teaching students from K–12 (and beyond) the issues that they need to be aware of when using technology. Technology continues to change, but with a good, grounded idea of the issues, the lessons learned can transcend these changes. Education is a process and everyone needs to begin with a good basis on which they can build.

CHAPTER 4

Professional Development Activities in Digital Citizenship

Before technology leaders begin to integrate digital citizenship into their school or district, faculty and staff should be trained on the appropriate use of technology. To do this, ongoing staff development activities covering the various areas of digital citizenship should be provided, along with informational resources to help participants understand the concepts.

This chapter provides 16 activities designed to give teachers, staff, and administrators a better understanding of digital citizenship and its implementation in a school or district. Many of the activities include links that lead to resources for staff development in technology. Staff developers are encouraged to use these resources to develop innovative ways to engage staff in the issues of digital citizenship.

Some of these activities are technologically based, while others are more traditional. The technology leader should keep in mind that some teachers, administrators, and parents may be facing a double learning curve—being exposed to the technology itself for the first time while also learning about the principles of digital citizenship. Technology leaders should choose activities that will keep users in their comfort zone until they are ready for stronger challenges.

Each activity is correlated to appropriate performance indicators from the International Society for Technology in Education (ISTE) National Educational Technology Standards for Teachers (NETS•T) and Administrators (NETS•A). Both sets of standards are listed in Appendix C.

Standard 5 of the NETS for Students and Standard 5 for Administrators, both called "Digital Citizenship," and Standard 4 for Teachers, "Promote and Model Digital Citizenship and Responsibility," all provide valuable starting points for considering appropriate uses of technology. Each of these sets of standards (updated respectively in 2007, 2009, and 2008) include the words "digital citizenship." By adding this language to their definition of technology standards, ISTE has shown how important they consider this topic to be in the professional development of teachers and administrators as well as in the education of students. Technology leaders need to provide this information to their constituents to explain why digital citizenship is important and how it can fit within the curriculum.

Activity Format

These activities are formatted to identify key objectives, points of emphasis, activity progression, and target outcomes. The format includes the following six elements:

Activity Title, NETS Addressed, Focus Question, and Related Questions. These are the elements of digital citizenship the activity is designed to explore.

Objective. The desired outcome of the activity is listed here.

Resources Needed. Resources include the tools and materials needed to complete the activity.

Activity Description. This section offers a step-by-step plan for answering the focus question and meeting the activity's key objective.

Extension Ideas. Educators can refer to these related activities for further professional development on the topic.

Teaching Tips. Here you'll find suggestions for working with teachers on digital citizenship.

Introduction to Digital Citizenship

The following activity is designed to introduce the basic concept of digital citizenship.

ACTIVITY 1 • Email Bingo (General Digital Citizenship)

NETS ADDRESSED NETS•T 4.b; NETS•A 5.c

FOCUS QUESTION How can we use technology to learn about the appropriate use of technology?

RELATED QUESTIONS Where can users learn digital citizenship concepts beyond just having technology training?

Can technology help to extend administrators' ability to teach new concepts to teachers?

OBJECTIVE Members will learn about appropriate uses of technology in a nonthreatening way.

RESOURCES NEEDED Icebreakers and Energizers: www.kimskorner4teachertalk.com/classmanagement/ icebreakers.html

Icebreakers, Warmups, Energizers, and Deinhibitizers: www.wilderdom.com/games/Icebreakers.html

Digital Citizenship Bingo cards (see Figure 4.1)

ACTIVITY DESCRIPTION Using the Digital Citizenship Bingo cards as an example, make a set of bingo cards with the entries in different locations. Distribute the bingo cards to your faculty.

Explain that you will be sending emails with concepts related to the digital citizenship elements. When an email has ideas related to an element, participants can mark it on their bingo card. Have them send an email to the technology leader once someone has a bingo (horizontal, vertical, or diagonal).

Keep a stash of prize incentives and distribute them to the winners. After someone has a bingo, announce that participants should clear their cards and start again.

EXTENSION IDEA Have faculty members come up with their own bingo cards for their classrooms. Find out how students respond to the activity.

TEACHING TIPS Make sure that the faculty members understand that this is to be a fun activity, but also one that will help them learn more about the elements of digital citizenship.

Have the faculty get together and share what they have learned by playing bingo.

Understand that some users may not be as interested in playing the game. If you make it interesting, people will follow.

DIGITAL ACCESS	DIGITAL RIGHTS & RESPONSIBILITIES	DIGITAL HEALTH & WELFARE
DIGITAL COMMUNICATION	DIGITAL LAW	DIGITAL COMMERCE
DIGITAL LITERACY	DIGITAL SECURITY	DIGITAL ETIQUETTE

Figure 4.1 Digital Citizenship Bingo: Nine elements students should know.

This activity can be tied to a book study that you might be doing on digital citizenship (see Book Study Bingo card example, Figure 4.2).

Know your audience—bingo activities may not be for every group.

We have put technologically driven change in a compartment so that traditional instructional activities can continue untouched.	… no generation has ever had to face the amount of change as those in the past 30 years have.	Due to the emergence of these new technologies, learning will not be confined to a single place or single source.	Paradigm is a model, perspective, value system, frame of reference, filter, or worldview that guides one's actions.
When two or more … technologies converge and blend, they create technological hybrids whose power is greater than the … individual technologies themselves.	Change is a subtle thing. Change is sneaky.	People do not need to know what the data says; they need to understand its impact and significance so it can become information.	Communication technologies will create even more global competition … for just about anything we can and cannot imagine.
In other words, schools have opted for trying harder with what is rather than working smarter with the new technology.	The ability to adjust, adapt, and leverage what you know will matter as much as the experience you have gained.	Is technology really changing our lives in fundamental ways, or is it merely being used to speed up old and outdated ways of doing things?	We should never limit our focus by looking only at what is "hot" today.
To fully appreciate the impact of technology on modern life, it is important to understand the development of technology throughout history.	Today, learning has become a lifelong process.	Educational institutions know that they must find solutions to this technology dilemma if they are to stay competitive.	It is really about seeing the present as nothing more than the past of the future.

Figure 4.2 *Windows on the Future* Book Study Bingo.
(Source of phrases: *Windows on the Future: Education in the Age of Technology* by Ted D. E. McCain and Ian Jukes, ©2001. Reprinted with permission of Corwin Press.)

Learning and Student Performance

Activities 2–8 are designed to help participants explore appropriate technology use while getting acquainted with otherwise unfamiliar technologies.

ACTIVITY 2 • Understanding Digital Technologies (Literacy)

NETS ADDRESSED	NETS•A 5.b; NETS•T 4.b
FOCUS QUESTION	How do educators teach students to use digital technologies?
RELATED QUESTIONS	Why is it important for teachers, students, and parents to have activities to learn about using technology?
	How can users of technology best learn about the issues surrounding the use of technology?
OBJECTIVE	Educators will discover new ways for teaching content using digital technologies.
RESOURCE NEEDED	Cyberlearning World—Bookmarks: First Day of School Icebreaker Activities: www.cyberlearning-world.com/nhhs/html/firstday.htm
ACTIVITY DESCRIPTION	Begin the session by dividing class members into groups of three or four.
	Ask the members about any interesting things they have done or heard of teachers doing through the use of digital technologies.
	Have the groups come up with three activities that they could do to teach the use of technologies to other teachers, to students, and to parents.
	Bring the groups back together and have them share their ideas.
EXTENSION IDEA	Have group members brainstorm technology activities they could do in their classes. Have them provide reasons why these activities would make the lessons more meaningful.
TEACHING TIPS	Identify areas where there are lots of ideas, as well as areas that need to be better represented.
	Allow members to be creative and come up with new and interesting ways to teach about appropriate technology uses, but require them to be specific about how they will accomplish these activities.
	Make sure that the group understands what would be considered good classroom activities.

ACTIVITY 3 • Appreciation Blog (Communication)

NETS ADDRESSED   NETS•A 5.d; NETS•T 4.d

FOCUS QUESTION   How can we use technology to recognize staff members for taking better advantage of the technology resources available to them?

RELATED QUESTIONS   Can technology help staff members feel more appreciated in their job?

Is technology an appropriate tool to help increase communication between staff members?

OBJECTIVE   Teachers will become more comfortable using digital technologies to communicate and collaborate with colleagues toward common goals.

RESOURCES NEEDED   Articles about "Employee Recognition": http://humanresources.about.com/lr/employee_recognition/123196/1/

Five Tips for Effective Employee Recognition: http://humanresources.about.com/od/rewardrecognition/a/recognition_tip.htm

ACTIVITY DESCRIPTION   Create a blog (see A Primer on Blogs, next page, for more information) to identify a staff member who has done exceptional work. Provide a professional biography of that staff member and explain why that person has been identified.

Ask users to reply to a blog entry and add their own personal information about this individual. If this is done by nomination, get the person who is nominated to contribute to the blog as well.

If time allows, design this activity so that all staff members can add new names to the teacher "blog of fame" whenever an individual does something that should be recognized. This update may be weekly, monthly, or at some other designated time.

EXTENSION IDEA   Begin posting school information on the blog. Invite the staff to respond to an entry on the blog.

TEACHING TIPS   Help instructors understand that blogs are a way to make the staff and community feel more connected.

Be careful when determining who can add information to the blog. Restricting write access to the blog may be important. However, allowing parents and students to have read access to the blog may also be a good thing. If you open the blog to outside readers, make sure to let the staff know so they can self-monitor what they post on the blog.

A Primer on Blogs

The word *blog* originated from a shortening of the phrase "web log." The most simplistic view of a blog is that it is an online diary. A large number of blogs are just that—an individual's account of his or her day, pets, relationships, or opinions about current events. But blogs can be much more than this. Because many allow readers to post comments and all allow entries to be linked to by other bloggers, the "blogosphere" is a communal space that promotes and sustains dialogue among any number of users with common interests.

This creates many opportunities for education and collaboration. If guided and encouraged correctly, students can use blogs to write stories, gather information, share data, and negotiate differing opinions and disagreements. Teachers and administrators can use blogs to share information with parents, make announcements, or create a forum for discussion.

The following lists provide several links related to blogs. The best way to learn about blogs, however, is to visit one (or several) and see what people are writing about.

Education Blogs

Online Education Database:
> http://oedb.org/library/features/top-100-education-blogs

The Landmark Project's Class Blogmeister:
> www.classblogmeister.com
> *Blogmeister allows educators to take a look at student blogs before they post.*

Weblogg-ed:
> www.Weblogg-ed.com

Other Blog Directories

(Note: Some material on these websites may not be suitable for all users.)

Blogged Directory:
> www.blogged.com/directory/education/k-12-education/

ontoplist.com's Education Blog Directory:
> www.ontoplist.com/education-directory/

Articles about Blogs in Education

Blogging 101:
> www.unc.edu/~zuiker/blogging101/

Using Blogs in the Classroom:
> http://husd4-tr.blogspot.com

ACTIVITY 4 • New Digital Communication Models (Literacy)

NETS ADDRESSED	NETS•A 5.d; NETS•T 4.d
FOCUS QUESTION	Why are blogging, podcasting, and Twitter important means of communication in a digital society?
RELATED QUESTIONS	Should teachers encourage the use of these technologies in their classrooms?
	Are these technologies appropriate for every classroom?
OBJECTIVE	Teachers and staff will learn about and experiment with the latest digital communication tools.
RESOURCES NEEDED	Landmarks for Schools: http://landmark-project.com
	Blogging Overview: http://robinfay.net/site/content/blogging-overview
	What Is Podcasting?: http://digitalmedia.oreilly.com/2005/07/20/WhatIsPodcasting.html
	Frequently Asked Questions about Twitter: http://support.twitter.com/forums/10711/entries/13920
ACTIVITY DESCRIPTION	Begin by asking what the group knows about blogging, podcasting, and Twitter (see Primers on pages 62, 64, and 66 for more information on these topics). Find out if teachers are already using any of these technologies in the classroom.
	Provide a basic introduction to these technologies, offering several educationally themed examples. After looking at these models, lead teachers in a discussion of how these technologies might be applied in their own classrooms.
	Ask the group to create a basic blog or podcast for school announcements or a blog for teacher support, and require all teachers to post at least a few comments or recordings over the next several weeks.
EXTENSION IDEAS	Once the podcast or blog is well established, publicize it to others in the school community (parents, administrators, students) as appropriate. Check the forum periodically to see how actively teachers are using these tools.
TEACHING TIPS	Provide teachers with user-friendly examples. Make their initial examples as simple as possible. Use terms and technical explanations that will be understandable to your audience.

A Primer on Podcasting

To understand podcasting, you first need to understand blogging (see A Primer on Blogs). In simple terms, podcasting is audio blogging. Instead of writing out information, podcasters record and post audio files on the Internet, where they are available for anyone who wants to listen to them.

Podcasting has its roots in the Apple community. The original podcasts were for Apple iPods, but today, any device that can play MP3 files can also play podcasts. The process for creating a podcast can be as complex or as simple as the user wants it to be. Several good audio editing programs are available that can help you make more professional-sounding recordings and eliminate the "ums" and mistakes. However the audio file is recorded, it needs to be saved or converted to the MP3 format. To learn more about creating a basic podcast and to find resources for doing so, see www.speedofcreativity.org/2006/02/28/podcast37-effective-school-podcasting/.

As always, the best way to learn a new skill is to use it. Even if you do not have an iPod or other MP3 player, most computers can play MP3 files. The Landmarks for Schools site (http://landmark-project.com) has several educational podcasts that you might find interesting.

What are the implications for education? Take a look at the Edupodder Weblog: http://Weblog.edupodder.com/2004/11/podcasting-in-education.html. The author, Steve Sloan, explores the many ways that podcasting can support educational objectives: distance learning, additional support for special needs students, and make-up classes, among others.

ACTIVITY 5 • Twitter for Gathering Information (Literacy)

NETS ADDRESSED	NETS•A 5.d; NETS•T 4.d
FOCUS QUESTION	How can teachers automatically monitor and get the latest updates on current events or on a particular topic?
RELATED QUESTION	How can technology be leveraged to provide new content and resources to faculty at little or no cost?
OBJECTIVE	Teachers and administrators will learn about Twitter and its educational applications.
RESOURCE NEEDED	50 Ways to Use Twitter in Education: http://cooper-taylor.com/blog/2008/08/50-ideas-on-using-twitter-for-education/
ACTIVITY DESCRIPTION	Twitter is a free service and it is easy to set up an account for yourself (see A Primer on Twitter, next page, for additional information). By using a Twitter account teachers and staff can have access to resources from in the school or around the world. Once these accounts are set up teachers can search for their particular fields—literature, biology, history, and so on. With this access teachers can ask questions and can quickly receive answers from other users.
	A Twitter account can provide current school information. Encourage teachers and staff to become followers of the page to see updates, resources, or all-staff questions.
EXTENSION IDEAS	Have teachers share their favorite Twitter pages with one another. Vote for the best ones and post the list on a web page or blog.
TEACHING TIPS	Have teachers in the same subject area work together to set up their Twitter pages and search for others to follow on their subjects. Recognize that some teachers will be apprehensive about all the new, "geeky" terms, and be patient and supportive. Take time to explain how Twitter works and what it can bring to the classroom.
	Help teachers integrate the use of Twitter to support their classroom lessons. Have them talk about what they've done and what seems to work best on a regular basis.
	A school Twitter site can be a great way to persuade teachers to try the technology, but it must used on a regular basis or faculty will lose interest.

A Primer on Twitter

Once users have an understanding of blogs, they are ready to move on to Twitter. Twitter is a micro-blogging site. It allows users to post short messages (or tweets) of 140 characters or less. The origin of Twitter started with cell phones (this is the reason for the short number of characters) but has grown beyond the original concept.

Major newspapers (such as the *New York Times*) and other traditional media outlets have created Twitter accounts to promote their content. Once you have set up your account with Twitter, any feeds that you subscribe to (or follow) will send updates directly to your account.

Creating an account is a simple process. Go to the site twitter.com and click on the Sign Up button to create an account. The site also has good primer information about using their service. Go to http://twitter.com/education to see some of the many examples.

The nice thing about Twitter is that users are able to ask questions and they will often receive information from other users in a matter of minutes (possibly less, depending who is online). Users can receive tweets from several different sources to stay updated about changes that are happening locally or around the world. Twitter is not one directional—users can become involved in the conversation.

The benefits for education are obvious. Teachers can subscribe to feeds on topics they are currently covering in class and receive the latest information as it happens. Schools can also create their own Twitter page for teachers, parents, and students, eliminating the need to send out hundreds of emails.

Here are some other excellent resources for learning about Twitter:

Clif's Notes—Twitter in Education:
http://clifmims.com/blog/archives/187

WeFollow—Education Twitter Users:
http://wefollow.com/twitter/education

Scribd—Can We Use Twitter for Educational Activities?:
www.scribd.com/doc/2286799/Can-we-use-Twitter-for-educational-activities

ACTIVITY 6   •   Blogs and Wikis for Parent Communication (Communication)

NETS ADDRESSED	NETS•A 5.d; NETS•T 4.d
FOCUS QUESTION	How can teachers use blogs and wikis to communicate classroom activities and events?
RELATED QUESTIONS	What benefits can these communication models have in a classroom?
	How can technology help parents become more involved in the learning process?
OBJECTIVE	Teachers will create a blog or wiki to share what is happening in their classroom with parents.
RESOURCES NEEDED	Social Media Explorer—Determining the Top Education Blogs: www.socialmediaexplorer.com/social-media-marketing/determining-the-top-education-blogs/
	Wiki in Education: http://c2.com/cgi/wiki?WikiInEducation
ACTIVITY DESCRIPTION	Introduce the concepts of blogs and wikis to teachers (see A Primer on Wikis, next page).
	Help teachers create a study guide for their classes, using a blog or wiki. The study guide should be made available to students and parents, and regularly updated and modified as the course progresses.
	Have teachers share their experiences with the study guide and ideas for improving it in follow-up staff meetings.
	Invite parents to visit these sites to see what their students are doing in class and to keep up-to-date on their progress.
EXTENSION IDEA	Create a moderated blog site and have teachers post ideas, questions, and thoughts about teaching with technology.
TEACHING TIPS	Make sure that teachers know enough about these tools to explain their use to students. Provide several examples.
	Communicate your expectations on frequency of posting—once a day, week, month, or any interval you think is appropriate.
	Underline the importance of articulating boundaries for appropriate postings: no profanity, no bullying, and so on. Teachers should remind students that parents will be looking at these sites.
	Inform parents and administrators that teachers will be using these tools in class, and ask them to support it with their involvement. Provide parents with a copy of the school or district acceptable use policy and show how this activity integrates with it.

A Primer on Wikis

According to one wiki information site:

> Wiki is Hawaiian for "quick." Wiki is also a software tool that allows users to freely create and edit hyperlinked web pages using a web browser. Wiki [software] typically uses a simple syntax for users to create new pages and crosslinks between pages on the fly. In addition to the main open source version there are also many non-commercial and commercial clones and some "wiki farms" (places where you can set up a wiki without needing your own server). (Blanche, 2004)

The wiki is a powerful tool for collaboration. One user can begin the development of a document or information page, and then other users can add to or make modifications to that document. A record of all changes and additions is kept (along with who made them). The most famous example of a wiki is the online encyclopedia Wikipedia: http://en.wikipedia.org.

Wikis can be used in classrooms for creating collaborative writing projects. For example, students can create their own study guides for the class. One student places some information on the wiki and others can update that information or add their own. Students can create a glossary of key terms, a timeline of critical events, a catalogue of important characters, or a list of essential formulas. Because the wiki resides on the Internet, it is always available to students and their parents.

Wikis require a bit more time and computer savvy than blogs or podcasts, but they can offer amazing returns in student learning and motivation when used well.

Wiki Resources

PBworks—Using PBworks in Education:
   http://pbworks.com/content/edu+overview

WetPaint—Wikis in Education:
   http://wikisineducation.wetpaint.com

ACTIVITY 7 • Use of Technology in Education (Literacy)

NETS ADDRESSED	NETS•A 5.b; NETS•T 4.a
FOCUS QUESTION	How can technology be effectively integrated in the curriculum?
RELATED QUESTIONS	What resources do teachers need to successfully use technology in their classroom?
	How can technology be used beyond typing papers and doing research on the Internet?
OBJECTIVE	Teachers will explore new ways to use technology to support content learning and personal productivity.
RESOURCES NEEDED	Microsoft.com—Lesson plans: www.microsoft.com/Education/en-us/teachers/plans/Pages/index.aspx
	Education World—The Concept-Mapping Classroom: www.education-world.com/a_tech/tech164.shtml
ACTIVITY DESCRIPTION	Ask teachers to describe how they currently use technology in their classrooms. Then, have them brainstorm ways they might use technology if no limitations were placed on equipment or access.
	Compile a list of the top ideas, and have teachers rank them by instructional effectiveness.
	As a group, identify which of these ideas could be accomplished right now in your school or district, given the technology resources currently available.
	Identify ideas that teachers could accomplish if they had more training in the technology involved.
EXTENSION IDEA	Ask teachers to prepare one lesson in the next two weeks that integrates a new technology. Have them report on their experience at a follow-up meeting.
TEACHING TIPS	Provide examples of innovative uses of technology in education.
	Provide teachers with a range of ideas, from the basic transfer of assignments (creating a movie instead of a paper, for example) to major changes in curriculum.
	Encourage teachers to look for new ideas and approaches instead of just updating activities they have used in the past.

ACTIVITY 8 • Providing Digital Access Outside School (Access)

NETS ADDRESSED	NETS•A 4.b; NETS•T 5a
FOCUS QUESTION	What kinds of digital access do students have outside school?
RELATED QUESTIONS	How many students have access to digital technologies outside school?
	What responsibilities do schools have to provide technology to students?
OBJECTIVE	Teachers and staff will better understand the technologies available to students outside school and will determine whether more school-sponsored access is needed.
RESOURCES NEEDED	Project Tomorrow—Speak up 2009 Report: www.tomorrow.org/speakup/pdfs/ SU09NationalFindingsStudents&Parents.pdf
	Digital Access Project: www.digitalaccess.org
	Digital Divide.org: www.digitaldivide.org
ACTIVITY DESCRIPTION	Invite teachers to poll the students (formally or informally) about the technology access they have outside school. Determine how much access is available outside school.
	Share the data on student access with teachers and administrators. Identify issues that might affect student learning.
	If a significant number of students do not have access to technology outside school, determine ways the school (or community) might help provide that access (e.g., by opening the school computer lab during evenings and weekends or partnering with community leaders to increase access at libraries and computer clubs).
	Have teachers discuss whether the lack of technology access is an issue for their classrooms. Are students assigned classroom activities that require technology access outside school? How does this affect their lessons?
EXTENSION IDEA	Discuss whether a 1-to-1 program (using laptops or handhelds) makes sense for your school or district. How might such a program be implemented and funded?
TEACHING TIPS	Have teachers evaluate their current practices and lessons in relation to technology access. Are they getting the most out of the technology they have available? Could greater student access make a difference in what they could do?
	If teachers are assigning projects that require technology access outside school, ask them to develop alternative assignments for students without access.

School Environment and Behavior

Activities 9–13 directly address appropriate and safe uses of technology.

ACTIVITY 9 • Appropriate Technology Use (Rights and Responsibilities)

NETS ADDRESSED   NETS•A 5.c; NETS•T 4.c

FOCUS QUESTION   Should students be able to use cell phones and digital cameras whenever and wherever they want?

RELATED QUESTION   When using digital technologies, what rights and responsibilities do people have?

OBJECTIVE   Teachers will gain a greater understanding of when and where it is appropriate to use technology in a school setting.

RESOURCES NEEDED   Group Icebreakers:
http://wilderdom.com/games/Icebreakers.html

Business Training Works:
www.businesstrainingworks.com/Train-the-Trainer/Icebreakers-Free.html

ACTIVITY DESCRIPTION   Begin a session on digital citizenship. A couple minutes into the presentation, have a teacher stand up and start taking pictures of all participants with their cellphone. A couple minutes later, have one teacher call another on a cell phone and begin a conversation.

Stop the session and have the teachers discuss their thoughts on these digital technology disruptions. Ask the teachers when it might be appropriate to use digital cameras or cell phones in the classroom and when it might not.

EXTENSION IDEA   Have the group come up with a set of rules to govern cell phone use during the school day.

TEACHING TIPS   Have teachers brainstorm ways digital cameras and cell phones might be used in the classroom to support learning.

Research your school or district AUP or look at the AUPs of similar schools and districts, and share these definitions of appropriate use with teachers. What modifications might be useful and appropriate?

Focus the discussion on appropriate use, rather than simply on restricting use.

ACTIVITY 10 • Inappropriate Technology Use (Rights and Responsibilities)

NETS ADDRESSED	NETS•A 5.c; NETS•T 4.c
FOCUS QUESTION	What criteria can be used to determine whether technology is being used inappropriately?
RELATED QUESTIONS	Why should we be concerned with the inappropriate use of technology? How can technology users come to agree on appropriate technology use?
OBJECTIVE	Teachers will explore different perspectives on appropriate and inappropriate technology use.
RESOURCE NEEDED	TeacherVision.com—Getting to Know Your Students: www.teachervision.fen.com/students/resource/2878.html
ACTIVITY DESCRIPTION	Have teachers write down the top three examples of what they consider inappropriate use of technology in the classroom. Compile these examples into a single list, and have the group vote on the top three issues. As a group, identify strategies for dealing with these issues, using a teaching solution.
EXTENSION IDEA	Ask teachers to implement this teaching solution in their classrooms, and report back on its effectiveness in limiting inappropriate use among students.
TEACHING TIPS	Ask teachers to provide a detailed rationale for why they consider these issues to be so important. Help participants eliminate what might be an individual class's concern, and focus instead on major concerns that affect the school or district as a whole.
	Focus on solutions to the issues rather than the issues themselves.
	Provide an opportunity for all participants to share their concerns, no matter how small they might seem.

ACTIVITY 11 • Digital Etiquette Issues (Etiquette)

NETS ADDRESSED	NETS•A 5.c; NETS•T 4.c
FOCUS QUESTION	Are there times that technology should not be used?
RELATED QUESTIONS	How do users decide when to use technology?
	How can users mitigate the possible negative effects of their technology use on others?
OBJECTIVE	Teachers will be sensitized to the emerging rules of etiquette that govern technology use.
RESOURCES NEEDED	NetM@nners.com: www.netmanners.com
	RudeBusters!: www.rudebusters.com/etitech.htm
ACTIVITY DESCRIPTION	Divide teachers into groups. Have them share examples of occasions when they were annoyed by someone else's use of technology, and explain what they did in these situations.
	Encourage the groups to come up with appropriate responses to these provocations and examples of bad "digital manners."
	As a larger group, discuss how good digital manners can be taught to students and enforced throughout the school community.
EXTENSION IDEA	Revisit this topic several months later. Ask teachers what they have done with their students to improve digital etiquette and what effect it has had on actual behavior.
TEACHING TIPS	Provide teachers with policies or procedures that other schools or districts have used to handle these issues. Determine whether they could work in your school or district.
	Provide examples of ways that certain situations could be handled. Discuss instances where the response is worse than the infraction. Have teachers come up with a better response.
	Discuss how particularly thorny issues (such as cell phone use) can be handled without simply banning the technology.

ACTIVITY 12 • Digital Citizenship and the District AUP (Rights and Responsibilities)

NETS ADDRESSED NETS•A 5.b; NETS•T 4.c

FOCUS QUESTION How do technology use problems within a school rank compared with other problems?

RELATED QUESTION How do we teach students technology rights and responsibilities in a school setting?

OBJECTIVE Teachers and administrators will work to improve their AUP to support digital citizenship efforts and priorities.

RESOURCES NEEDED About.com—Acceptable Use Policies: http://compnetworking.about.com/od/filetransferprotocol/a/aup_use_policy.htm

Education World—Getting Started on the Internet: Developing an Acceptable Use Policy (AUP): www.education-world.com/a_curr/curr093.shtml

ACTIVITY DESCRIPTION As a group, review your school or district AUP. If your school or district does not have one, find examples from other schools or districts and share them with the group.

Discuss whether having an AUP alone will eliminate the problems with technology use that your school or district is currently experiencing.

Distribute the Survey for Digital School Issues vs. Nondigital School Issues (see page 75). Have participants rank the list of issues from 1 (the least important issue currently facing the school) to 9 (the most important issue).

After completing this survey, distribute the Ranking for Digital School Issues vs. Nondigital School Issues (see page 76). Have participants rank all the issues on a scale of 1 to 5 (5 being extremely important and 1 being extremely unimportant).

Discuss your scores as a larger group and determine issues that deserve immediate attention, and where technology use fits into those priorities.

EXTENSION IDEA Have the administrators look at AUPs from several different schools. Evaluate how they could be used to improve your own AUP, or whether entirely new policies are needed.

TEACHING TIPS Discuss with administrators the policies governing technology use in the school or district. Are these policies teaching appropriate use of technology or are they just attempting to restrict technology use in the school?

Review your school or district AUP with legal counsel. Can these policies be defended in a court of law?

Survey for Digital School Issues vs. Nondigital School Issues

Instructions. Considering all issues faced by administrators and staff, which of the following are most important or least important to our school? Rank them from 1 (least important) to 9 (most important). Do this for the digital issues first, then for the nondigital issues.

Digital Issues

_____ A. Tunneling around school firewall

_____ B. Using text messaging during class

_____ C. Playing games on laptops, netbooks or celluar devices during class

_____ D. Using cell phones during class

_____ E. Accessing pornographic websites on campus

_____ F. Failing to use technology effectively and to its fullest extent

_____ G. Using social networking sites or texting to intimidate or threaten other students

_____ H. Illegally downloading music files from the Internet

_____ I. Plagiarizing content or information obtained online

Nondigital Issues

_____ A. Stealing school property

_____ B. Vandalizing school property

_____ C. Using drugs or alcohol on campus

_____ D. Skipping classes

_____ E. Bringing weapons to school

_____ F. Bullying or hazing

_____ G. Treating teachers and administrators with disrespect

_____ H. Cheating on assignments or tests

_____ I. Fighting on school property

Ranking for Digital School Issues vs. Nondigital School Issues

Instructions. Rank the following issues from 1 to 5 (5 being extremely important and 1 being extremely unimportant).

Issue	Extremely Important	Somewhat Important	Neither Important nor Unimportant	Somewhat Unimportant	Extremely Unimportant
Using drugs or alcohol on campus	5	4	3	2	1
Tunneling around school firewall	5	4	3	2	1
Fighting on school property	5	4	3	2	1
Using text messaging during class	5	4	3	2	1
Stealing school property	5	4	3	2	1
Playing games on laptops, netbooks, or cellular devices during class	5	4	3	2	1
Vandalizing school property	5	4	3	2	1
Using cell phones during class	5	4	3	2	1
Skipping classes	5	4	3	2	1
Accessing pornographic websites on campus	5	4	3	2	1
Hazing	5	4	3	2	1
Underutilizing technology resources	5	4	3	2	1
Cheating on assignments or tests	5	4	3	2	1
Using social networking or texting to intimidate or threaten students	5	4	3	2	1
Bringing weapons to school	5	4	3	2	1
Illegally downloading music files from the Internet	5	4	3	2	1
Treating teachers and administrators with disrespect	5	4	3	2	1
Plagiarizing information obtained from the Internet	5	4	3	2	1

ACTIVITY 13 • Protecting Personal Security (Security)

NETS ADDRESSED	NETS•A 5.b; NETS•T 4.a
FOCUS QUESTION	How can technology users protect their personal security?
RELATED QUESTIONS	What security issues do people need to be aware of when using technology?
	How can technology users ensure that personal information remains secure?
OBJECTIVE	Teachers will gain a better understanding of the issues of personal privacy in a digital society.
RESOURCES NEEDED	AntiOnline: www.antionline.com
	National Cyber Security Alliance—StaySafeOnline.org: www.staysafeonline.org
ACTIVITY DESCRIPTION	Divide the large group into several smaller groups. Each group should designate a group leader to lead them in discussing and identifying 10 things they do to protect themselves (or others) while using technology.
	Create a list of security activities that group members are currently engaged in. Have them create a list of additional things they could do to make themselves and others safer.
	Have each of the groups write their lists on large pieces of paper and post them in the room. Each group should explain their list to the larger group. Identify common themes, both in what is currently being done and what should be done in the future.
EXTENSION IDEA	Have teachers report back at the next gathering on any new efforts they have taken to improve the security of their (or their students') personal information.
TEACHING TIPS	Some users may not understand the difference between digital security (antivirus and spyware programs, surge or power protection, password protocols, encrypted data and Internet communications, etc.) and digital health and wellness (protecting the physical and psychological well-being of the user). Be sure to clarify these differences at the outset.
	Provide opportunities for all group members to participate. Do not allow one person to monopolize the activity.

Student Life Outside the School Environment

Activities 14–16 focus on appropriate digital technology outside an academic setting.

ACTIVITY 14 • Digital Rights Management (Law)

NETS ADDRESSED   NETS•A 5.b; NETS•T 4.a

FOCUS QUESTION   What is Digital Rights Management (DRM)?

RELATED QUESTION   Why is Digital Rights Management important for schools?

OBJECTIVE   Teachers and administrators will learn about DRM and its effect on schools.

RESOURCES NEEDED   American Library Association—Digital Rights Management: www.ala.org/ala/issuesadvocacy/copyright/digitalrights/

Electronic Privacy Information Center— Digital Rights Management and Privacy: www.epic.org/privacy/drm/

ACTIVITY DESCRIPTION   Divide participants into groups. Aim for a mix of technology skill levels in each group. Have groups research current initiatives related to Digital Rights Management. Ask them to summarize their findings and explain them to the whole group.

After the groups have researched the topic and defined DRM, have them discuss the positive and negative effects of DRM on technology use in the school.

Discuss as a large group how current practices in schools should be modified in response to DRM.

EXTENSION IDEA   Have the teachers take these ideas back to their classrooms and ask students to discuss how they would be affected by their implementation.

TEACHING TIPS   Allow an opportunity for teachers to share their views and biases on the subject. Help them to distinguish between facts, feelings, and opinions. Clear up any misconceptions about DRM.

ACTIVITY 15 • Buying Items Online (Commerce)

NETS ADDRESSED NETS•A 5.b; NETS•T 4.a

FOCUS QUESTION What do users need to know when buying items online?

RELATED QUESTION Why should teachers be concerned with online purchasing?

OBJECTIVE Teachers will learn more about the many ways that items are bought and sold on the Internet.

RESOURCES NEEDED CNET News—Tips for Safe Online Shopping: http://news.cnet.com/8301-19518_3-10405719-238.html

Privacy Rights Clearinghouse—Online Shopping Tips: E-Commerce and You: www.privacyrights.org/fs/fs23-shopping.htm

Microsoft Safety and Security Center— How to shop online more safely: www.microsoft.com/security/online-privacy/online-shopping.aspx

Be Safe Online—Shopping Online: www.besafeonline.org/English/shopping_online.htm

ACTIVITY DESCRIPTION Ask teachers how many have purchased items online. Then, ask them if they have personally had (or have heard about) problems with online purchases. Have teachers share these experiences.

Have teachers do an informal poll of their students to get an idea of how actively they are buying and selling things online, and what problems they have encountered. Have teachers report this data back to the group and generate a master list of problems and issues encountered when purchasing things online.

Discuss with the group the pros and cons of teaching students about safe and informed online purchasing.

EXTENSION IDEA Have teachers go back to their classrooms and work with students to generate a list of dos and don'ts for making purchases online. Share these lists with the wider school community.

TEACHING TIPS Provide resources that will help teachers and students research and recognize the reputability of a site. Define terms that might not be common vocabulary (e.g., secure site, PayPal, online auction). Make sure teachers understand the basics before they work with their students on digital commerce issues.

Prepare to have some teachers identify this as an area that should not be part of the curriculum. Discuss the similarities between this issue and teaching sex education or a healthy diet.

To demonstrate the importance of this topic, provide teachers with statistics on identity theft, the amount of money spent online by teenagers, and changing consumer practices.

ACTIVITY 16 • Technology Addiction (Health and Wellness)

NETS ADDRESSED   NETS•A 5.b; NETS•T 4.a

FOCUS QUESTION   How can students become addicted to digital technology?

RELATED QUESTION   What can teachers do to identify technology addiction?

OBJECTIVE   Teachers will gain a greater awareness of the signs and dangers of technology addiction.

RESOURCES NEEDED   Psychology Today—Techno Addicts:
www.psychologytoday.com/blog/brain-bootcamp/200907/techno-addicts

Computer Weekly—
Technology Addiction Disrupts Teenagers' Learning:
www.computerweekly.com/Articles/2009/09/10/237643/Technology-addiction-disrupts-teenagers39-learning.htm

ACTIVITY DESCRIPTION   Survey students about their technology use, both in school and out. Include in this poll questions about time spent online, time spent with video games, cell phone usage, and other pertinent topics.

Share this information on the technology habits of students with staff. Have teachers discuss whether they see this pattern of use as a problem for student engagement or performance in school.

Work with counselors to identify students who may be having issues with technology addiction. Have them share that information with teachers.

Devise a plan for working with parents, teachers, and students on the topic of technology addiction.

EXTENSION IDEAS   Provide workshops for parents on the potential problems with technology addiction.

Provide ways to help parents identify and address the issue, and offer support mechanisms for teachers who believe they may have students with addiction problems.

TEACHING TIPS   Identify strategies to support the use of digital technology without encouraging overuse.

Define technology addiction and describe how it differs from normal use. Without this information, teachers may become overly concerned about what may just be typical technology use.

STUDENTS

Section III
Digital Citizenship in the Classroom

*Education makes machines which act like men
and produces men who act like machines.*

—ERICH FROMM

Students need to be educated on how to be good citizens of their country and what their rights and responsibilities are as members of that society. The same issues need to be addressed with regard to the emerging digital society, so that students can learn how to be responsible and productive members of that society. By teaching students about the nine elements of digital citizenship, you prepare them to enter that world with confidence and a good ethical direction.

All educators are well aware of the many challenges that teachers currently face: increased high-stakes testing; a bewildering array of national, state, and local standards; new demands for higher qualifications and recertification. Given these challenges, it is difficult to find time to teach even core subjects, much less anything new. This is why a detailed understanding of the nine elements of digital citizenship (and the issues that accompany them) will help educators recognize the "teachable moments" that may occur as they are working with other content, and use those moments to reinforce digital citizenship principles. When discussions about technology use arise, digital citizenship can act as a cornerstone of that discussion.

This section provides teachers with ideas and activities they can use to raise student awareness and to teach the principles of digital citizenship in the classroom. The lesson plans in the following chapters can be modified for students at all grade levels and can form the foundation of a comprehensive digital citizenship program.

5

Teaching Digital Citizenship to Students

When helping students with the issues of digital citizenship, teachers should strive to bolster each student's ability to:

- Live in a world saturated with digital technology

- Understand appropriate technology use

- Use technology skills for their future

I've created a reflection model as a teacher resource to help students begin thinking about how they are using technology—not just in school, but in their homes and with their friends. This model should be followed each time a student uses a technology. As students become more aware of their actions, the principles embedded within this model will become mental habits that will inform the way students use digital technologies now and in the future.

The reflection model has four stages (see Figure 5.1):

1. Awareness

2. Guided practice

3. Modeling and demonstration

4. Feedback and analysis

Teachers can use this reflection model to help focus student understanding of appropriate technology use in a learning environment.

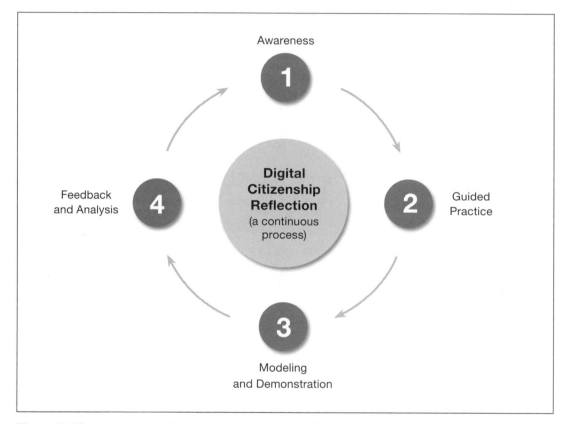

Figure 5.1 Four-stage reflection model for teaching digital citizenship.

Stage 1: Awareness

Awareness focuses on helping students become technologically literate. The awareness stage goes beyond just basic knowledge of hardware and software, however necessary these skills are. Teachers need to engage students in discussions about the appropriate use of these digital technologies. Students should be encouraged to ask themselves:

- Do I have a good understanding of how a particular technology works and how using this technology can affect me as well as others?

- Have I learned about the potential problems or issues related to using this technology?

- What rules (legal and ethical) govern the acceptable use of this technology?

The activities in Chapter 6 can help students understand the differences between using digital technology in acceptable ways and misusing or abusing digital technology.

Stage 2: Guided Practice

Following instruction in awareness, teachers should lead students in guided activities that help them recognize and practice appropriate use. Give students an opportunity to learn these principles in an atmosphere where exploration and risk taking are promoted. During this period, students will need the teacher's support and understanding when mistakes are made.

As much as possible during this guided practice phase, allow students to use the same technologies in the classroom as they do outside of school. While this may seem to be an invitation to chaos, it really isn't. Students need guided practice for learning digital citizenship skills, and where better than the classroom? Without guided practice, inappropriate use of technology can occur without students being aware of it. Students need to have an opportunity to learn the skills in a safe environment.

Quick Lesson: Role-Playing with Cell Phones

Have students role-play situations using cell phones in a public location (e.g., in a movie theater). The cell phone usage here should be conducted in a loud and obtrusive fashion. Pose the following question after the role-playing activity: What would be the appropriate way to respond to this situation?

Teachers can use the following questions to help students reflect on how they use technology:

- When I use technologies, do I recognize when there is an issue of inappropriateness? Why or why not?

- Have I considered the appropriateness of my actions? Why or why not?

- Can I differentiate examples of technology misuse and abuse? Why or why not?

- What do I need to do to become aware of my actions when using technology?

Stage 3: Modeling and Demonstration

Teachers should next offer students explicit "modeling lessons" that focus on appropriate technology use in the classroom. It goes without saying, of course, that teachers should practice the same good digital citizenship habits as they advocate. For example, teachers who use cell phones should turn them off or put them on vibrate during class. If students are not allowed to answer or make cell phone calls during the day, then teachers should follow those same rules.

Parents can also be enlisted to help teach digital citizenship. Sending home digital citizenship lessons and having parents engage in the same dialogue with their children can be a great way to reinforce digital citizenship principles. Adults need to be positive role models of good digital citizenship so children can follow their example.

Quick Lesson: Reviewing the School's AUP

Have students discuss what is considered technology misuse and abuse in your school or district, as defined by your AUP. Ask them to provide examples of appropriate and inappropriate use, and articulate the differences between them.

Finally, students should be led to an understanding of cause and effect with regard to technology use. All forms of technology use, misuse, and abuse have consequences. Teachers should model appropriate technology use on a regular basis. While doing so, teachers should focus on the following questions:

- Am I violating laws, policies, or other codes by using technology in this way? Why or why not?

- Have I seen, read, or heard of similar situations? What were the consequences?

- Does digital citizenship provide direction for determining the appropriateness of my actions? How? Why?

Stage 4: Feedback and Analysis

The classroom should also be a place where students can discuss their use of technology inside and outside of school, to see how they can use it more effectively and appropriately. Encourage students to analyze and explore why they should use technologies in a certain way. Provide feedback that will help students find ways to avoid or mitigate problems that may arise from inappropriate technology use.

It can be difficult to "go back" and think about one's actions after they occur. Without the opportunity to self-reflect, however, inappropriate behavior will tend to be repeated over and over. Students need to reflect on their actions and ask themselves:

- Am I satisfied with my decision? Why or why not?

- Am I satisfied with the outcome of the situation? Why or why not?

- Did my behavior have a positive or negative influence on others? Why?

- Did I go back and evaluate how I used the technology later?

- Did I think about possible alternatives of how to use the technology?

Incorporating Digital Citizenship into the Curriculum

Digital citizenship should become a priority for schools. All stakeholders—administrators, board members, teachers, parents, and students—need to be involved in a continuous dialogue about the appropriate use of technology. It should be clear to all that being a good citizen is just as important in the digital world as it is in the "real world."

Digital citizenship principles should be taught at all levels and should be integrated into all subjects. As such, teaching digital citizenship as a planned part of the curriculum underscores the message that using technology is a privilege and not a right.

The time to start teaching digital citizenship is now. Technology misuse and abuse is widespread and occurs inside and outside school. Although AUPs are important, they are not enough. Students must learn what is appropriate and inappropriate—an understanding that comes through discussion and dialogue, not just by following a set of rules.

The next time you hear a cell phone ring in a movie theater or at school, ask yourself if that person is a responsible digital citizen or yet another example of an uneducated technology user. Then remind yourself that it doesn't have to be this way.

CHAPTER 6

Foundational Lessons in Digital Citizenship

Despite media stories to the contrary, not all young people today are savvy users of technology. Some students have considerable experience with blogging, podcasting, text messaging, and cell phone use, while others have little or no experience with digital technologies. The problem is compounded by the fact that most students have never been taught the appropriate use of technology, and even fewer understand the potential implications of using that technology.

In this chapter, I present five foundational lesson plans that teachers can incorporate directly in their classroom to teach the fundamental principles of digital citizenship. Directions and materials are provided to help teachers and students get started. The objective is to encourage students and teachers to consider how to use technology appropriately, and to create a comfort level with the ideas of digital citizenship. Once this comfort level has been reached, teachers can move on to the more technology-rich lessons in Chapter 7.

At the end of this chapter, a scoring rubric has been provided to help teachers assess how well their students have understood the topics presented. The rubric is not meant to be a grading tool. Instead, it is a way to benchmark how the students are following the topics.

Each lesson includes correlations to the refreshed ISTE National Educational Technology Standards for Students (NETS•S) and for Teachers (NETS•T). The full text of these standards is provided in Appendix C. Digital citizenship primarily involves the fifth standard in the NETS for Students ("Digital Citizenship") and the fourth standard in the NETS for Teachers ("Promote and Model Digital Citizenship and Responsibility").

The NETS provide a valuable starting point in learning about appropriate uses of technology. The new NETS have become refocused to provide performance indicators for each group. These new NETS provide a direction for educators on how to present technology to students.

Digital citizenship should not be seen as something separate from student technology use in the classroom, but as an integral part of the learning process. The next generation of technology users will be faced with these issues every day of their lives. Students need to learn appropriate technology use not just for the classroom, but also to be good technology-using citizens for life.

Lesson Format

The format for each lesson includes the following six elements:

Lesson Title, NETS Addressed, Focus Question, and Related Questions. These are the elements of digital citizenship that the activity is designed to explore.

Objective. The desired outcome of the activity is listed here.

Resources Needed. Resources include the tools and materials needed to complete the activity.

Activity Description. This section offers a step-by-step plan for answering the focus question and meeting the activity's central objective.

Extension Ideas. Educators can refer to these related activities to extend the lesson.

Teaching Tips. Here you'll find suggestions for working with students on digital citizenship.

FOUNDATIONAL LESSON 1 • Appropriate or Inappropriate Use?

NETS ADDRESSED	NETS•T 4; NETS•S 5
FOCUS QUESTION	How can students determine whether they are using technology appropriately?
RELATED QUESTIONS	What information do students need to know to use technology appropriately?
	How can students evaluate whether their use is appropriate?
OBJECTIVE	To help students recognize situations involving inappropriate technology use.
RESOURCE NEEDED	MindTools—Decision Making Techniques: www.mindtools.com/pages/main/newMN_TED.htm
ACTIVITY DESCRIPTION	Organize students into groups of two or three to ensure that all members have an opportunity to contribute to the discussion.
	Provide each group with a different technology use scenario (see Technology Use Scenarios, 1–17, next pages). Have group members discuss the scenario. After they have discussed the scenario, have them decide:

- Is the individual using technology inappropriately?

- What actions make the scenario appropriate or inappropriate?

- What could or should the individual have done differently?

Have each group report their conclusions to the class.

EXTENSION IDEAS	Have students come up with their own scenarios of appropriate or inappropriate technology use and share them with the class.
	Have students draft acceptable use polices for the classroom based on the elements of digital citizenship. Start by having students review the acceptable use policy of your school or district. Have students work in pairs or groups and then have them create a new set of policies as a class.
TEACHING TIPS	Provide guidance as necessary to help students who may not have been exposed to or know enough about a particular technology to make an informed decision.
	Make sure that students understand that each scenario can be viewed in different ways. If students have a difference of opinion, open it up to the whole class for discussion.

Technology Use Scenarios

Scenario 1. Sean decides to create a website that is a parody of his school's website. Sean uses the same website style as the school, but makes up stories and misinformation about the school, such as features about weekend drinking parties. Because he is in the class that makes changes to the real website, he is able to direct people to his website instead of the real one. The principal, Ms. Martinez, finds out about the change when an angry parent calls to complain about a story on the website mentioning her daughter. Ms. Martinez contacts the school technology support person, Mr. Jones, and requests that he remove the parody site. She also asks Mr. Jones to find out who is responsible.

Scenario 2. Michelle likes to go to her Facebook site. Often she will spend two or three hours each day on Facebook. She has a friend list of over 200—some are close friends but others are just friends of friends. She updates her status several times a day and goes to many friends' sites as well. Michelle's mom thinks that she has about 20 friends on Facebook. What issues might this cause?

Scenario 3. Sarah received a cell phone for her birthday. As with most cell phones, hers has the ability to take photos and video. During algebra class, she decides to take a picture of Ms. Everett, the substitute, while her back is turned to the whiteboard. When she gets home she downloads the picture then uploads it to her Facebook site and talks about how boring class was. What are the issues?

Scenario 4. During word processing class, Mr. McIntosh notices that Mary has both of her hands under the computer desk. As Mr. McIntosh comes around to her station Mary puts her hands back on the keyboard but he notices that her cell phone is on her lap with a text on the screen. Mr. McIntosh asks Mary to stay after class, where she says that she was sending a text to her mother about picking her up after school. What does the teacher do?

Scenario 5. Tim and his friends spend a lot of time working on computers and they understand how to get around security features. Tim decides to see how far he can get into the school's computer system. Tim manages to get onto the school's server and decides to change a few grades for his friends, "just for the fun of it." The next day a rumor is circulating that someone has hacked the school's server. That afternoon, Tim is called to the office to talk to the principal.

Scenario 6. John and his friend Mike both have camera phones. Mike sits in the back of the class and uses his phone to photograph the test for John, who is taking the test that afternoon. Mike then emails the photograph of the test to John's phone.

Scenario 7. Mrs. Peters enjoys working with technology. She has been working with computers for several years now and has her own website to allow friends to keep up with what her family is doing. Every year she posts her family's holiday photo on the website. A friend who lives overseas contacts her and says that she saw her family's photo being used as an advertisement. Neither Mrs. Peters nor her husband know anything about it. How do you protect your identity?

Scenario 8. Mr. Scott, principal of Rural High School, is walking through the library and sees a student working on a computer. Strolling by, he sees that the student is on a music site that requires a credit card to purchase music. Mr. Scott informs the student that the district's acceptable use policy does not allow buying items online using school computers.

Scenario 9. Jamie has persuaded her parents to let her talk to her friends in an online chat room. Many of the people in the chat room are Jamie's friends, but there are some people she does not know. For several days, she has noticed one of these individuals talking to some of her friends. Now, this person is starting to ask Jamie about herself and what she looks like. Jamie becomes uncomfortable and logs off the chat room. Later that evening, she talks to her parents and mentions the person in the chat room and how it made her feel.

Scenario 10. Kevin has just purchased the latest video game, *Too Fast '22*. He and his friends enjoy playing games on the computer. His best friend Vince also likes to play video games, but doesn't have the money to buy the latest games. Kevin decides to be a good friend and give a copy of the game to Vince.

Scenario 11. Mrs. Smith considers herself to be a pretty savvy computer user. She has been working with computers for five years and uses them regularly in class. Mrs. Smith gets an email from someone she does not know but opens the email anyway. When she opens it, the message has some advertisement for a free gift, so she deletes the email. Several days later she is working on her computer and notices that her Internet browser is working very slowly. She decides to check the computer with an antivirus program and discovers that she has a virus on her computer. She determines that the virus came from the email she received several days previously.

Scenario 12. Matt enjoys taking pictures with his digital camera. His pictures are quite unusual and can be easily identified as his work. He wants to let other people see his pictures so he posts them on his website. A couple of months later he is surfing the Internet and sees some of his pictures on someone else's website. At first he is flattered that someone enjoyed his pictures, but on closer inspection he sees that he is not credited anywhere on the site as the person who took the photos. The way the images are posted makes it seem as if the site owner had taken the pictures.

Scenario 13. Dr. Brown, principal at Bluebird Elementary School, is concerned with safety in his school, both for his staff and for students. During the summer, Dr. Brown had cameras installed in each of the classrooms. The video from each of these cameras is viewable on the Internet, so that parents can check on their students' classes during the day. Some parents are concerned that because these cameras are connected to the Internet, other people could also use them to "spy" on their children.

Scenario 14. Mr. Hutchinson wants to keep his students' parents aware of classroom activities. He remembers hearing about blogs at a technology conference. After doing some research, Mr. Hutchinson finds both positive and negative viewpoints related to using blogs in the classroom. He believes that for what he wants to do—inform parents of their child's daily work—a blog would be appropriate. Before setting one up, however, he consults with the principal and technology support person to see if there are any legal issues. Both say that what he wants to do is perfectly okay. Mr. Hutchinson then sets up a blog and informs his students and parents about where to find the information.

Scenario 15. Max is always on the computer. Except when he is at school, Max is on his social networking sites, video sites, or just surfing websites. He communicates with many people using his social networking sites or texting but rarely leaves the house. His mother is becoming concerned that he is not seeing his friends or going out. What should Max's mother do?

Scenario 16. Kelly just got her driver's license. Her parents allow her to take the car to school and to her part-time job. She enjoys the freedom of being able to drive. One night, her parents allow her to pick up her friend Sally to go to the movies. She begins driving to Sally's house and remembers she wanted to remind her other friend Lisa that they were meeting after the movie. She decides that she can text Lisa and continue to drive to Sally's house. Kelly gets so involved with typing the text to Lisa that she does not see the car ahead of her braking. At the last minute, she is able to step on the brakes and stop her car before becoming involved in an accident. What went wrong?

Scenario 17. Ms. Deal does not like having several passwords for all her accounts. Because she has so many she gets into the habit of writing the passwords on a sticky note on her monitor so she won't forget. While she is out of her office, John, a student who had been in trouble in her class earlier in the day, comes by her office. He sees the passwords and writes down the one for Ms. Deal's email account. John goes to another computer, logs in as Ms. Deal and sends several insulting emails to other staff members. How could this have been avoided?

FOUNDATIONAL LESSON 2 • Digital Compass

NETS ADDRESSED	NETS•T 4; NETS•S 5
FOCUS QUESTION	Do students think about technology use differently than adults?
RELATED QUESTIONS	How do we begin the discussion with students on what should be considered appropriate or inappropriate use of technology?
	When should students learn about appropriate technology use?
OBJECTIVE	To have students think about where they are with respect to technology usage.
RESOURCE NEEDED	Maricopa Center for Learning and Instruction— Warm-Up Activity: www.mcli.dist.maricopa.edu/show/what/warmup-act.html

ACTIVITY DESCRIPTION

Divide students into groups of two or three. Provide each group with a digital compass (Figure 6.1) and the list of 12 scenarios (Digital Citizenship and the Digital Compass Activity, next page).

Instruct groups to discuss each of the 12 scenarios and identify what direction they believe the individuals in the scenarios are going in terms of technology use. Group members should also come up with one or two scenarios of their own and identify their direction on the compass as well.

Have students explain their results and give reasons for why they chose a particular direction for each scenario.

Discuss the six directions on the compass and find out how well the students understand each of the directions.

Follow up with a discussion of how students, as technology users, should begin to think about the ways they use technology in school and elsewhere.

EXTENSION IDEAS

Have students (individually or in groups) create additional scenarios of appropriate and inappropriate technology use. Then have the class determine where they would place these scenarios on the compass.

Have students come up with appropriate punishments or consequences for scenarios that are clearly inappropriate.

TEACHING TIPS

Prepare to have students view these scenarios differently than most adults, and ask them to carefully articulate their reasoning.

Some students will find it difficult to see the effect that inappropriate technology use can have on others. Work to make it clear to students how inappropriate activities affect others.

Know that some students will choose a particular position just to get attention from others. Make sure students can explain why they are taking that position.

Digital Citizenship and the Digital Compass Activity

Directions. Give each student a copy of the Digital Compass or display a copy. Read the following scenarios. Instruct students to decide which direction of the compass matches the technology use described in the scenario. After everyone has made a choice, have students analyze their answers.

Scenario 1. A student sends a harassing text message to another student. The receiving student retaliates with their own maltreatment text. *How should sending harassing and retaliation text messages be dealt with?*

Scenario 2. When hanging out with friends, one student gets a cell phone call and conducts a conversation within the group. *What is the proper etiquette when using a mobile phone in a public place?*

Scenario 3. A student logs on to a file-sharing website and downloads the newest song. *When is downloading music from a file-sharing site appropriate?*

Scenario 4. A student follows a questionable link to a website and downloads a malicious script that releases a virus on the school network. *Should users take time to verify questionable links before downloading material from unknown sites?*

Scenario 5. An hour before class, a student remembers that a writing assignment is due. The student goes to the library, logs on to a website, and copies and pastes information without giving credit to the authors. *What are the issues of using Internet materials without giving credit to the authors?*

Scenario 6. At home, a student uses a software package to copy movies and games for friends. *What should be considered when duplicating copyrighted materials?*

Scenario 7. A student downloads a proxy tunneling program to their school computer to circumvent the schools' firewall. *Should students use software to "tunnel" around the schools' firewall to get to the sites they want?*

Scenario 8. Two students use text messaging on their cellular phones to pass information during class. *Is it wrong to send text messages during class?*

Scenario 9. The school administration places all the enrollment documents on the school website. *Is it right to assume that all homes have access to Internet access?*

Scenario 10. A student brings a USB flash drive to school with all the student's assignments. The student checks with the teacher before connecting the drive to the school's computer. *Is it appropriate for students to connect their own hardware to school computers?*

Scenario 11. During class, students use their cellular phones to share answers to an assignment. *Is it wrong to use personal cellular devices to work on assignments during class?*

Scenario 12. Students obtain a copy of the final exam from the teacher's computer by using the teacher's password. *Is using the teacher's credentials to get to information wrong?*

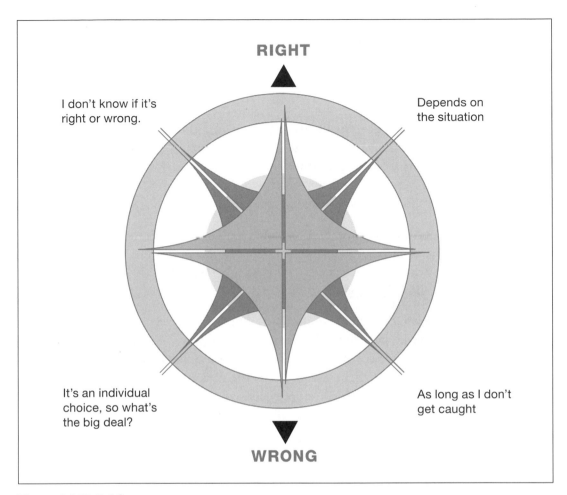

Figure 6.1 Digital Compass.

Interpreting the Answers

There is no easy answer for any of the scenarios. Student responses will vary. Why? Technology users are not always going to agree on what is right and wrong. When using technology, there are often shades of gray that can be interpreted in a number of different ways. When evaluating each scenario, users need to consider not only their feelings but the feelings of other users around them. Some users may have had poor role models, developed bad habits, or perhaps lack the ability to think before acting. The purpose of this compass activity is to help students analyze their ideas about appropriate technology use. The six directions of the compass vary from due north, Right, to due south, Wrong.

Wrong. When users travel in the wrong direction, it's often because of bad information, a lack of training, or a lack of consideration for others. To get back on the right path, students need to learn how their technology use can affect others.

It's an individual choice, so what's the big deal? Often students don't consider how others may feel about their behavior, and they believe "If it doesn't bother me, why should it bother anyone else?" Students traveling in this direction can't understand what the fuss is all about. Teachers need to help these students see beyond their own experiences.

As technology becomes more personalized and accessible, it becomes a part of who we are, for better or worse. Students may express the opinion that "Because my cell phone is mine, then what I do with it is only my concern." Be prepared to compare personal technology use to other, similar activities, such as driving a car or wearing inappropriate clothing to school.

As long as I don't get caught. Students choosing this direction believe that technology is there to be used and everything will be fine as long as no one else knows. The trouble with this attitude is that what we do or do not do can and often does affect others around us. Many students know that what they are doing is not right, but they believe that if no one knows, that makes it okay.

Depends on the situation. Some situations do lend themselves to varying interpretations, but an overarching understanding of appropriate technology use is still important. There are times when a student needs to know that some activities may be appropriate in one situation and inappropriate in another.

I don't know if it's right or wrong. Some students are given technology but are not trained (or fail to learn) how to use it appropriately. However, ignorance of the rules cannot be used as a defense for technology misuse or abuse. Basic digital citizenship skills should be learned when using technology. This is the direction students go when they understand some aspects of technology but only enough to be dangerous. Sometimes, this can be worse than having no training at all. When no digital citizenship training is provided, students learn from others and can get poor advice.

Right. Traveling in the right direction takes time and diligence. To follow this path, students need to have a good understanding of the technology they are using. They also need to reflect on how they use technology on a daily basis. Those who follow the right direction take time to decide not only how their actions affect themselves, but also those around them.

FOUNDATIONAL LESSON 3 • Recognizing the Nine Elements of Digital Citizenship

NETS ADDRESSED	NETS•T 4; NETS•S 5
FOCUS QUESTION	Can students identify the main ideas behind each of the nine elements of digital citizenship?
RELATED QUESTIONS	How well do students know the nine elements of digital citizenship?
	Why are these nine elements important?
OBJECTIVE	To make students more aware of the many different aspects of digital citizenship.
RESOURCES NEEDED	Ribble, M., Bailey, G., & Ross, T. (2004). Digital citizenship: Addressing appropriate technology behavior. *Learning & Leading with Technology, 32*(1), 6–11.
	Ribble, M., & Bailey, G. (2004). Digital citizenship: Focus questions for implementation. *Learning & Leading with Technology, 32*(2), 12–15.
ACTIVITY DESCRIPTION	Spend some time introducing and discussing the nine elements of digital citizenship.
	Pass out the Digital Citizenship Matching Activity (next page) to assess students' understanding of the nine elements. Use the results to identify the areas that need to be addressed in more detail.
	Identify any problems that students may be having with a particular element. If a large number of students are not able to identify that element, plan further activities to reinforce the principles involved.
EXTENSION IDEA	Have students come up with their own examples of appropriate and inappropriate use for each of the nine elements.
TEACHING TIPS	Reinforce that the nine elements are designed to clarify the range and interaction of issues that can be placed under the umbrella of "digital citizenship." Help students identify the issues that affect them most.
	Prepare to have students locate some issues in more than one element, and assure them that there is overlap between elements. Often this is because digital technologies have multiple functions.
	Help students make the connection between the elements of digital citizenship and future work or personal interactions.

Digital Citizenship Matching Activity

Instructions. Match the examples of technology use with the matching element of digital citizenship.

Examples of Technology

1. ___ Leaving private information open on social networking sites

2. ___ Talking loudly on a cell phone in a public place

3. ___ Fully understanding how a technology is to be used

4. ___ Having up-to-date virus protection, firewalls, and surge (or battery) protection

5. ___ Requiring everyone to get information from a website

6. ___ Understanding how to research and network to get the best deals online

7. ___ Using ergonomic chairs, desks, and other furniture and equipment to minimize physical harm

8. ___ Downloading illegally obtained material from the web (e.g., music from some file-sharing sites)

9. ___ Protecting the identity of others and yourself online

10. ___ Using a blog to share personal information with others

11. ___ Creating a wiki site to share information happening in the classroom

12. ___ Spending many hours a day on the Internet

Element of Digital Citizenship

a. Digital etiquette

b. Digital communication

c. Digital literacy

d. Digital access

e. Digital commerce

f. Digital rights and responsibilities

g. Digital law

h. Digital health and wellness

i. Digital security

Answer Key for Matching Activity

1. **f**   Leaving private information open on social networking sites

2. **a**   Talking loudly on a cell phone in a public place

3. **c**   Fully understanding how a technology is to be used

4. **i**   Having up-to-date virus protection, firewalls, and surge (or battery) protection

5. **d**   Requiring everyone to get information from a website

6. **e**   Understanding how to research and network to get the best deals online

7. **h**   Using ergonomic chairs, desks, and other furniture and equipment to minimize physical harm

8. **g**   Downloading illegally obtained material from the web (e.g., music from some file sharing sites)

9. **f**   Protecting the identity of others and yourself online

10. **b**   Using a blog to share personal information with others

11. **c**   Creating a wiki site to share information happening in the classroom

12. **h**   Spending many hours a day on the Internet

Holistic Score. The holistic score provides a general level of online computing usage and understanding. Look at your holistic score and the description of that score below.

0–4 This score shows minimal understanding of the elements of digital citizenship. You need to look closer at the use of digital technologies and their effect on society.

5–9 This score shows basic understanding of digital citizenship. Although you have some knowledge of the elements, more investigation is needed.

10–12 This score shows substantial knowledge of digital citizenship. You know and understand digital technology and how it relates to the larger society.

FOUNDATIONAL LESSON 4 • Digital Driver's License

NETS ADDRESSED	NETS•T 4; NETS•S 5
FOCUS QUESTION	What should students know about appropriate use before they are allowed to use technology at school?
RELATED QUESTION	When should students begin to learn about the appropriate use of technology?
OBJECTIVE	To ensure that students have basic competency in the nine elements of digital citizenship.
RESOURCES NEEDED	PBS Kids GO! —Webonauts Internet Academy: http://pbskids.org/webonauts/
	Atomic Learning—Tech Skills Student Assessment: www.atomiclearning.com/k12/en/assessment
ACTIVITY DESCRIPTION	Administer the Digital Driver's License Exam (next pages) for the particular level you are teaching (elementary for Grades 4–6, secondary for Grades 7–10). Students must complete the exam with an 80% or better score to be considered eligible for a license.
	Students who have passed the exam should be allowed to tutor those with less satisfactory scores until they are able to pass the exam.
EXTENSION IDEAS	Have students create their own exam questions. Use these questions to further discussion of digital citizenship issues.
	Have students create a technology "driving" test that would serve as a companion to this written exam. Have students identify which skills would be most important for success in the school environment.
TEACHING TIPS	Work with students prior to giving the exam to help them identify appropriate and inappropriate uses of technology.
	Show students that learning how to use technology appropriately is to their advantage; the more informed they are, the more protected they will be from possible problems.
	Remind students that, just like driving a car, technology use is a privilege, not a right, and that users must follow the "rules of the road" to retain that privilege.

Elementary Digital Driver's License Exam

Digital Manners (Etiquette)

1. Having your cell phone turned on during school hours is
   a. a bad idea because it might disturb others.
   b. a good idea for keeping in touch with parents.
   c. no big deal because everyone else does it.
   d. your choice if it doesn't affect anyone else.

Digital Messages (Communication)

2. When writing on a social networking site (such as Facebook), should you share your secrets?
   a. Sure, a social networking site is like a diary, so this is where I should put them.
   b. It doesn't matter. Only my friends read my page.
   c. No, the social networking site is often open to anyone who has access to the Internet.
   d. Sure, as long as no one knows my true identity.

Digital Learning (Literacy)

3. When learning about technology in school, it is important for you to know
   a. the rules for using technology.
   b. how to work with others when using the technology.
   c. how different technologies are used.
   d. all of the above.

Digital Inclusion (Access)

4. Students with disabilities (those who aren't able to see, hear, or walk)
   a. can't use technology.
   b. should have the same opportunities as others to use technology.
   c. are not able to understand and learn about technology.
   d. have no reason to use technology.

Digital Business (Commerce)

5. If your parents allow you to buy things on the Internet, you should
   a. think twice about buying online, because all sites are dangerous.
   b. follow what your friends say about where to buy.
   c. find the first site that has what you want and buy it.
   d. first check to see if the site is safe and secure when buying something.

Digital Trust (Law)

6. When looking at graphics and text from the Internet
   a. take whatever you want because that's the purpose of the Internet.
   b. ask your friends for places to find material you can copy.
   c. ask for permission to use the information before using it.
   d. avoid it because all information on the Internet is false.

Digital Privileges (Rights and Responsibilities)

7. When using a new technology in class, you should
   a. do whatever you want because no one ever checks.
   b. ask teachers and parents about what can be done.
   c. figure out ways that you can have fun with it.
   d. ask your friends because they know about technology.

Digital Protection (Health and Wellness)

8. How I work with technology (e.g., sitting, lying, stooping at the desk, floor, or sofa)
   a. doesn't matter as long as I am comfortable.
   b. depends on where I am.
   c. isn't something that I need to be concerned about.
   d. shouldn't be ignored.

Digital Precaution (Security)

9. When dealing with people online, giving personal information is
   a. okay as long these people live far away.
   b. never a good idea, no matter the reason.
   c. fine as long as the people are nice.
   d. nothing to worry about.

Answer Key for Elementary Digital Driver's License Exam

1. a Many schools allow students to have cell phones in school for safety, but require that they be turned off or silenced during the school day. This keeps students focused on doing the right things in school.

2. c Social networking sites are often open to anyone on the Internet. Many users think that they are like diaries and that students should share their most personal thoughts on their page. Social networking sites can be useful tools to share information, but users need to be careful what they share.

3. d Technology affords many opportunities for students to learn beyond the classroom. But there must be an understanding of how to use the technologies first.

4. b Students with disabilities should have opportunities to work and learn with technology. Some students may need special technology tools to provide this opportunity (e.g., screen readers, special input devices, speech-to-text converters).

5. d Purchasing goods and services online needs to be taken seriously. People can gain information about you and your family from information that you provide. Make sure the site is secure by checking it over. (For example, does it have secure access only, does it ask only questions that are appropriate for the purchase, does it have alternate ways to contact the company?)

6. c Students need to realize that when "borrowing" anything from the Internet, its use is restricted by the owner (unless stated otherwise). All content taken from the web should be cited appropriately.

7. b All users have certain rights and responsibilities when using technology. It is important to know what is appropriate and what is not appropriate before using technology.

8. d Users often don't think about safe technology use habits until they hurt themselves. How you use technology today can have a big effect on how you will be able to use it in the future.

9. b It is easy to act differently online than face-to-face. Students need to make sure that private information remains private.

Secondary Digital Driver's License Exam

Digital Etiquette (the standards of conduct expected by other digital technology users)

1. During school hours the correct cell phone ringer setting is
   a. low.
   b. vibrate.
   c. specialized ring tone.
   d. high.

2. Netbook computers and smartphones should be used in class for
   a. exchanging ideas from class discussions.
   b. helping friends get the answers.
   c. playing games.
   d. sending notes during a teacher's lecture.

Digital Communication (the electronic exchange of information)

3. Email messages should be
   a. long and full of details.
   b. sent to as many recipients as possible.
   c. short and to the point.
   d. sent without a subject line.

4. Texting can be a good tool for
   a. sharing what happened in class with friends.
   b. discussing class topics.
   c. talking to friends when bored in class.
   d. inviting people outside the school into the discussion.

Digital Literacy (the ability to use digital technology and knowing when and how to use it)

5. The most appropriate use of technology in schools is to
   a. do research only.
   b. find resources to help learn the class topics.
   c. write class papers only.
   d. play games during class.

6. Online learning is
   a. difficult and not worth the time.
   b. not well understood by students.
   c. like trying to take a class without a teacher.
   d. being used in many school districts.

Digital Access (full electronic participation in society)

7. Assistive technologies for people with disabilities are
   a. necessary for some users to access information.
   b. seen as just an additional expense.
   c. expensive relative to regular technology.
   d. needed for a few students.

8. The differences between those with access to digital technology and those without is
   a. not a big deal because all technology is a luxury.
   b. something that can never be fixed.
   c. a concern that needs to be addressed by the school or district.
   d. not a priority for the school or district.

9. Digital technology-based assignments should be
   a. avoided because some students may not have access to technology at home.
   b. integrated into the classroom.
   c. approached cautiously for fear of offending someone.
   d. assigned for out-of-class work only.

Digital Commerce (the buying and selling of goods online)

10. Purchasing goods and services online is
    a. a waste of time because selling goods on the Internet is a scam.
    b. something that everyone has learned at home.
    c. not a skill to be overlooked by schools.
    d. not needed by students in schools.

11. Searching for information about products online before buying is
    a. important if you are looking for the best price.
    b. too time consuming.
    c. a lot of work and usually not very informative.
    d. difficult because many products are not offered online.

Digital Law (the legal rights and restrictions governing technology use)

12. Information on the Internet is
    a. available for people to use as they want.
    b. copyrighted and should be treated as someone else's property.
    c. easy to copy and paste into your own document.
    d. unreliable and suspect.

13. Sharing music or copyrighted material online
    a. doesn't hurt anyone because musicians and actors make enough money.
    b. is the best way to deal with greedy companies.
    c. is illegal and should not be done.
    d. keeps the musician or actor popular.

Digital Rights and Responsibilities (the privileges and freedoms extended to all digital technology users, and the behavioral expectations that come with them)

14. If someone puts copyrighted material on the Internet and another person wants to use it, that person should
    a. use it, if it is for educational use.
    b. take it and use it as he or she wants.
    c. not use the information because it is probably inaccurate.
    d. ask permission from the author or at least cite the source.

15. In schools, students should
    a. have the ability to do whatever they want online.
    b. follow their school's acceptable use policies.
    c. look at other students' email if they have the password.
    d. come up with rules with their friends for using technology.

Digital Health and Wellness (the elements of physical and psychological well-being related to digital technology use)

16. Physical injuries related to technology use
    a. are not a major concern.
    b. will not happen for many years, so should not be a priority.
    c. can have dramatic and painful effects on your body.
    d. rarely happen at school.

17. Furniture and chairs for technology should be
    a. the right height and size for using that technology.
    b. any size because it doesn't matter to students.
    c. bigger than the students to allow them to stretch.
    d. soft and flexible so the students can be comfortable.

Digital Security (the precautions that all technology users must take to guarantee their personal safety and the security of their network)

18. When dealing with strangers, online users should
    a. give personal information freely.
    b. be cautious about giving information.
    c. provide passwords and credit information if asked.
    d. not tell anyone about people they meet online.

19. To protect a computer from viruses, a user should

    a. never open an email message.

    b. unplug the computer from the Internet.

    c. keep up to date virus definitions.

    d. trust the service provider to protect the computer.

20. Virus protection and firewalls are

    a. foolproof and never need to be checked.

    b. a waste of time and money because virus attacks only happen to big businesses.

    c. effective but not necessary.

    d. a good investment, but they need to be monitored and updated regularly.

Answer Key for Secondary Digital Driver's License Exam

1. b Vibrate is correct because it is the least distracting setting during the school day. Many schools allow students to carry cell phones for safety and security reasons. A specialized ring tone might be able to identify your phone from others but can be annoying to other users. Another option would be to turn off the phone during school hours.

2. a The ability to share information saved on a netbook computer or smartphone can lead to significant learning. But in a testing situation or when others are talking, handhelds should not be used this way.

3. c Email is intended for short communication. Long and involved emails are often either not read or filed for later review. A descriptive subject line can alert the user about the importance and content of the email.

4. b Students can use text messages to express themselves in a less threatening fashion. Texting is not a place to gossip, waste time, or exclude others from being in the conversation.

5. b Technology can be a helpful tool and can provide additional resources for teaching and learning. Technology can assist instructors to be more efficient in their teaching.

6. d Online learning is being used in many school districts in the U.S. Online learning, if done correctly, can be a great benefit for everyone who wants to become a lifelong learner.

7. a Some students (and adults) with disabilities need assistive technologies so that they can access digital information. Everyone should have an opportunity to access information. Many of these technologies are very cost effective.

8. c There is still a "digital divide" between those who have access to technologies and those who do not. Often basic technology needs go unfulfilled, even as prices decrease. As society becomes more technologically integrated, it will become the responsibility of the school to develop a plan for addressing this need.

9. b Some teachers are reluctant to assign technology-based assignments because some students might not have access (e.g., at home or at the library). These assignments should be integrated into the classroom where students have access to technology.

10. c Teenage students are becoming one of the largest groups of online consumers. It is important that they be protected from exploitation. The process of buying goods online needs to be taught and discussed.

11. a Technologies such as the Internet provide many tools for finding useful information. The Internet also offers the opportunity to buy and sell goods, but the smart shopper looks around to find the best value. With the search tools that are available today, finding a reliable vendor with good prices is quick and easy.

12. b According to copyright law, anything that is produced by an individual is copyrighted whether they have gone through the legal process or not. The Internet makes it easy to copy something and pass it off as original work, but this is plagiarism. Users also need to differentiate between real and fabricated information on the Internet. Much information is credible, but you cannot assume that it is credible without close examination.

13. c Downloading materials without an artist's consent is stealing. Most users know that taking files from the Internet is wrong, but rationalize it for a variety of reasons (e.g., high cost, availability).

14. d If material is copyrighted, users must give credit to the person who created it. If you are going to make a profit from a source, permission must be obtained. Educational users can have access to some copyrighted material, but the rules of copyright need to be thoroughly understood.

15. b Most schools have set up acceptable use policies for technology use in school. If someone is going to use technology appropriately, that person needs to follow the rules that have been created.

16. c Repetitive stress injuries happen after extended periods of using technology incorrectly. There are long-term effects, but there are also short-term effects that include fatigue, eye problems, and sore muscles.

17. a When purchasing technology, educators need to consider the environment in which students will use it. Furniture that is the wrong size or not made for the purpose it is being used for can make it difficult for students to use technology. It can also lead to technology-related injuries such as repetitive stress, eyestrain, and sore muscles.

18. b It can be very difficult to know who you are communicating with when using digital technology. It is easy to disguise your identity online. Be cautious about giving out personal information such as your home address or phone number. Do not give out information such as passwords or credit information.

19. c Protecting one's computer from a virus or Trojan horse attack takes diligence on the part of the user. It is necessary to maintain virus protection. You should not open emails or attachments from people you do not know.

20. d Virus protection, firewalls, surge protectors, and battery backups are all appropriate tools to help protect your technology investment, but purchasing them is not enough. These tools need to be monitored and updated to ensure they are working properly.

FOUNDATIONAL LESSON 5 • What Does It Mean to Be a Digital Citizen?

NETS ADDRESSED	NETS•T 4; NETS•S 5
FOCUS QUESTION	What is my responsibility as a digital citizen?
RELATED QUESTIONS	What do students need to know about technology use as a digital citizen?
	How can students become more aware of their place in a digital society?
OBJECTIVE	To raise student awareness of what it means to be a member of a digital society.
RESOURCES NEEDED	Digital Citizenship and Creative Content: http://digitalcitizenshiped.com
	Digi Teen—Digital Citizenship for Teenagers: http://digiteen.ning.com
ACTIVITY DESCRIPTION	Have students think about what it means to be a citizen of a city, state, or country. What can they do or not do as citizens?
	Ask students about the technologies they use to interact with other people. Could the people they interact with be considered a community? Are they citizens of that community?
	Discuss how a digital citizen should act when working with a group. Should there be rules of conduct? If not, why not?
	Have students think about their own use of technology and whether they always use it appropriately.
EXTENSION IDEA	Discuss one of the nine elements of digital citizenship in more detail, and explore how it affects users both in school and out.
TEACHING TIPS	Provide examples and scenarios that demonstrate appropriate and inappropriate use of technology (see Chapter 2).
	Make sure students understand how their actions can affect others in a digital society.
	Prepare for some students to disagree with you on appropriate use, and open a dialogue with them that illuminates both sides of the issue.
	Prepare to look at technology use from many perspectives. Instructors need to be flexible enough to see how students' use of technology may also be appropriate.

Scoring Rubric for Foundational Lessons

Use this scoring rubric to assess student comprehension of the topics presented.

OBJECTIVES	Exemplary Performance 4	At or Above Average 3	At or Below Average 2	Low Performance 1	Points Earned
Student has an understanding of the importance of the concept.	Student has a complete grasp of the concept.	Student is not sure about the importance of the concept.	Student is unaware of the importance of the concept.	Student does not understand the topic.	
Student is involved in the classroom activity.	Student is completely engaged.	Student is interested but not engaged.	Student is not providing effort in class.	Student is not interested in the topic.	
Student understands the relevance of the topic to the larger discussion of digital citizenship.	Student has a good grasp of both the topic and digital citizenship.	Student is aware of digital citizenship but unsure of the connection.	Student has only a minimal understanding of either the topic or digital citizenship.	Student does not understand either the topic or digital citizenship.	
Student can come up with related examples of topics within digital citizenship.	Student is able to use information from the activity to come up with new concepts related to digital citizenship.	Student can provide limited examples with prompting from the teacher or other students.	Student has difficulty making the connection between the activity and other examples.	Student is not able to come up with any examples beyond what is presented in the activity.	
Student understands the need to use technology appropriately.	Student makes the connection between appropriate technology use and good citizenship.	Student understands that technology should be used appropriately but believes that some misuse is okay.	Student is having difficulty realizing how inappropriate technology use affects others.	Student cannot understand the need for using technology appropriately.	
At the conclusion of the activity, did the student seem to gain any new ideas or concepts?	Yes, the student seemed to learn many new ideas.	Yes, the student took away some ideas.	Not sure.	No, the student seemed disinterested in the topic.	
Overall, what effort did the student put forth in this activity?	The student has given much effort to the topic.	The student worked hard, but not 100%.	The student did very little during this activity.	The student provided no effort in doing this activity.	
				TOTAL SCORE:	

Holistic Score. The holistic score provides a general level of understanding of the topic and digital citizenship. Look at the holistic score and the description of that score below.

25–28 Exemplary understanding of the topic and digital citizenship. Student has a good understanding of the concept.

22–24 Above average understanding of the topic and digital citizenship. Student understands the topic but still needs additional resources.

20–21 Average understanding of the topic and digital citizenship. Student needs more time to learn about this topic and the overall concept of digital citizenship.

17–19 Low understanding of the topic and digital citizenship. Student has little knowledge of the topic; more work is needed.

Below 17 Student has no understanding of the topic or is uninterested.

7

Guided Lessons in Digital Citizenship

Digital citizenship involves the appropriate use of all current digital technologies, as well as technologies that are still in development. Teachers need a number of resources to help them get started with digital citizenship, and the following 15 guided lesson plans are designed to help teachers engage students in the classroom.

Each lesson plan focuses specifically on one of the nine elements of digital citizenship (lesson themes are identified in the lesson title). These lessons can be easily customized to address specific student needs. Each lesson provides resources to help teachers modify it for their particular classes.

A scoring rubric is located at the end of the chapter to help teachers assess student comprehension of the topics presented. The rubric is not meant to be a grading tool. Rather, it is a benchmark to assess student understanding.

Lesson Format

The format for each lesson includes the following six elements.

Lesson Title, NETS Addressed, Focus Question, and Related Questions. These are the elements of digital citizenship the activity is designed to explore.

Objective. The desired outcome of the activity.

Resources Needed. Resources include tools and materials needed to complete the activity.

Activity Description. This section offers a step-by-step plan for answering the focus question and meeting the activity's central objective.

Extension Ideas. Educators can refer to these related activities to extend the lesson.

Teaching Tips. Here you'll find suggestions for working with students on digital citizenship.

Student Learning and Performance

Guided Lessons 1–6 address the communication, literacy, and access elements of digital citizenship.

GUIDED LESSON 1 • Cell Phone Interruptions (Communication)

NETS ADDRESSED	NETS•T 4.a; NETS•S 5.a
FOCUS QUESTION	Should people be able to use cell phones in public places?
RELATED QUESTIONS	Should cell phones be banned in certain places?
	Should only certain people be able to leave cell phones on (e.g., doctors, emergency workers, people with sick relatives)?
OBJECTIVE	To determine where cell conversations are appropriate.
RESOURCE NEEDED	The Let's Talk.com Cell Phone Etiquette Guide: www.letstalk.com/promo/unclecell/unclecell2.htm
ACTIVITY DESCRIPTION	Have pairs of students conduct mock cell phone conversations in front of the class in which they are being loud and talking about inappropriate topics. When the task is completed, have students describe what they heard. Have them explain how the exchange made them feel.
	Have students discuss their feelings as they spoke in front of the class. Ask if they have any problems having a cell conversation in other places (such as a place of worship or a movie theater).
EXTENSION IDEA	Have students discuss cell phone issues with their friends. Have them come back to class and share what they and their friends think about cell phone use in school and other public places.
TEACHING TIPS	Have students focus on positive ways to help cell phone users improve their cell phone etiquette.
	Coach students on appropriate cell phone usage in terms of both location and topics. Have students keep a journal on times they use the cell phone and have them reflect on why it may have been an issue in particular situations.
	Supply students with methods for dealing with inappropriate cell phone use. Yelling at or hushing cell phone users is usually not a good solution to the issue. Be a good technology role model for the students. Students will follow your example.

GUIDED LESSON 2 • Message Misinterpretation (Communication)

NETS ADDRESSED	NETS•T 4.a; NETS•S 5.a
FOCUS QUESTION	How can students avoid misunderstandings when using various communication technologies?
RELATED QUESTIONS	How can email and text messages be misinterpreted by receivers?
	What can students do to avoid miscommunicating their intentions when sending emails and text messages?
OBJECTIVE	To learn the correct way to write and interpret email and text messages.
RESOURCES NEEDED	Communication Factors in Email: http://strategyleader.org/articles/emailcommunication.html
	Hybrid Language: A Study of Email and Miscommunication: www.stc.org/confproceed/1998/pdfs/00090.pdf
ACTIVITY DESCRIPTION	Divide the class into two groups. Line up the two groups across from one another. Give every other person a small slip of paper and a pencil.
	Tell the first person in each group a sentence. For example, "The answer to the problem of miscommunication is to practice good digital communication and reflection."
	Instruct the first person in each group to write down the sentence and hand it to the next person. The second person must then recite the sentence to the third person, who then needs to write it down. Continue this process down the line.
	After the last person has heard the sentence, have that person write it down and give it back to the teacher. See how close each group comes to the original sentence.
	Discuss how difficult it can be to go from an oral message to a written one and back again. Talk about how messages can be misinterpreted or miscommunicated, especially when people are not in the same room.
EXTENSION IDEA	Have students share personal experiences with miscommunication using some technology (e.g., email, text message, or cell phone). Ask them to identify what they could have done differently to avoid the miscommunication.
TEACHING TIPS	Make sure that group members stand far enough away from each so they can't hear or see what their neighbors are doing.
	Make sure students recite the sentence with little inflection.
	Confirm that students see the correlation between this familiar exercise and the way that digital messages can become garbled.

GUIDED LESSON 3 • Using the Internet Appropriately (Literacy)

NETS ADDRESSED	NETS•T 4.a; NETS•S 5.a
FOCUS QUESTION	Do students know where to get quality information from the Internet?
RELATED QUESTIONS	What resources do teachers need to find quality information on the Internet?
	How should the Internet be used in the classroom?
OBJECTIVE	To improve student use of the Internet as a source of information for learning.
RESOURCES NEEDED	Kathy Schrock's Guide for Educators–Teacher Helpers: WebQuest in Our Future: The Teacher's Role in Cyberspace: http://school.discoveryeducation.com/schrockguide/Webquest/Webquest.html
	UC Berkeley—Evaluating Web Pages: Techniques to Apply & Questions to Ask: www.lib.berkeley.edu/TeachingLib/Guides/Internet/Evaluate.html
	WebQuest Portal: http://Webquest.org
ACTIVITY DESCRIPTION	Spend some time discussing the basics of performing an Internet search. Have experienced students help those who have not used a search engine before.
	Create an Internet scavenger hunt sheet and have students find sites that appropriately match the squares on the sheet.
	Provide prizes for those who successfully complete the scavenger hunt sheet.
EXTENSION IDEA	Create lessons in which students must find information on the Internet related to the subject. Have students explain why the information they found was appropriate for the lesson.
TEACHING TIPS	Develop your understanding of websites and the way they are organized so that you will be able to help students identify the source of the information (author, sponsor, etc.) and how recently it was updated.
	Teach students what to look for on a website to establish its credibility and accuracy.
	Realize that some students may have more experience in web searches than others. Make sure that one person does not dominate a group. Have everyone participate.

GUIDED LESSON 4 • How Do Businesses Use Technology? (Literacy)

NETS ADDRESSED   NETS•T 4.a; NETS•S 5.a

FOCUS QUESTION   Are businesses concerned about how workers (especially new workers) use digital technologies?

RELATED QUESTIONS   What legal, ethical, and productivity issues surround the use of technology in business settings?

Will these trends change in the future?

OBJECTIVE   To understand how businesses look at the appropriate use of technology in the workplace.

RESOURCE NEEDED   businessballs.com—Brainstorming Process: www.businessballs.com/brainstorming.htm

ACTIVITY DESCRIPTION Invite business leaders to the school and have them talk about the digital technology skills they use every day in their work. Focus on how they handle the appropriate use of technologies.

Have students create a list of the technology skills that are needed in business today, and have them speculate on skills that will be needed in the future.

EXTENSION IDEA   Have students ask their parents how they use technology in their workplace and if there are rules they must follow when using technology.

TEACHING TIPS   Interview potential business leaders prior to their visits and discover if they are using digital technologies in their businesses. Try to find progressive business leaders who want workers to use digital technologies.

Spend some time prior to the presentation to provide students with information about digital citizenship (if they are not already aware). This will help them focus their attention on appropriate technology use.

Make sure that students have prepared some basic questions on digital citizenship issues prior to the presentation(s).

GUIDED LESSON 5 • MP3 Files for Teaching (Access)

NETS ADDRESSED   NETS•T 4.b; NETS•S 5.b

FOCUS QUESTION   How can MP3 players be used to support teaching in the classroom?

RELATED QUESTIONS   Do students have access to the hardware and software they need to play MP3 files in the classroom?

Can audio files be used to extend instruction and help students learn better?

OBJECTIVE   To learn how MP3 files can be used to support instruction and learning.

RESOURCE NEEDED   Gary S. Stager—Podcasting in Education Resources: www.stager.org/podcasting.html

ACTIVITY DESCRIPTION   Survey students on whether they currently have an MP3 player or are planning to purchase one in the near future (see A Primer on MP3 Files and Players, next page). Ask them their opinion of podcasts, and find out whether they would use their MP3 players to listen to lectures, guest speakers, instructional commentary, or audio books (see A Primer on Podcasting in Chapter 4 for information on podcasting).

Ask students what other information or resources would be useful for their learning if they were digitally recorded.

Create instructional audio files and place them on a web server. After two weeks, find out the number of students using the MP3 files and whether these files are helping students in class.

EXTENSION IDEAS   Discuss with other teachers how podcasting might be used in their classrooms. Offer to help other teachers set up their own podcasts.

TEACHING TIPS   Identify whether there is an interest in (and an ability to access) MP3 files. If there is little interest or access, this may be of little help in the classroom.

Maintain the MP3 files so that they are up-to-date and relevant to what is happening in the classroom.

Inform the administration that you will be doing this activity. Because of the potential cost, inform parents that this activity is voluntary and that they do not need to purchase an MP3 player.

Prepare for some comments related to MP3 files and players being a fad. Make sure that you can explain how MP3 files can support teaching and learning.

A Primer on MP3 Files and Players

MP3 files are easy to download and share with other users. Typically, audio files are saved and shared using this format.

The *Encyclopedia Britannica* defines the MP3 file as the "standard technology and format for the compression of audio signals into very small computer files."

> For example, sound data from a compact disc (CD) can be compressed to one-twelfth the original size without sacrificing sound quality. Because of small file size and ease of production from CD sources, the MP3 format is very popular for transmitting music files over the Internet. (*Encyclopedia Britannica* Online, 2006)

Once audio files have been converted to this file type, they can be played on various digital technologies, such as computers, laptops, dedicated MP3 players, smartphones, netbooks, and tablet technologies. The large variety of devices that can play MP3 files has increased the number of people who can listen to them. There are certainly many different models and a price range of devices that can fit most budgets. One of the determining factors for choosing an MP3 player is the amount of memory it has; greater memory means more storage space for audio files. To find out more about the different types of players, go to CNET Reviews and locate the MP3 player review section: http://reviews.cnet.com.

Many people use MP3 players to listen to music, but other types of audio files can be played on them as well. Podcasts have become a popular source of information on almost any subject (for more information on podcasts, see A Primer on Podcasting in Chapter 4). Now that users, especially students, use their smartphones (and cell phones) to play all types of music and video files, this information is even more accessible. Educators are increasingly seeing the educational potential of podcasts for reaching students in new ways. To find educational podcasts, go to the Digital Podcast Website (www.digitalpodcast.com/browse-educational-20-1.html) and search under education.

GUIDED LESSON 6 • Bridging the Digital Divide (Access)

NETS ADDRESSED	NETS•T 4.a, 4.b; NETS•S 5.a, 5.d
FOCUS QUESTION	What effect does lack of access to digital technology have on student learning and performance?
RELATED QUESTIONS	What issues might come up when students have varying degrees of access to digital technology?
	What role should school districts play in providing access to all students?
OBJECTIVE	To make students more aware of the issues related to technology access.
RESOURCE NEEDED	PBS Teachers—Digital Divide Archive: www.pbs.org/teachers/learning.now/digital_divide/
ACTIVITY DESCRIPTION	Divide the class into three groups. Students in the first group are not given access to any computers; students in the second group have computers but no Internet access; students in the third group have computers with Internet access.
	Inform all three groups that they must write a one-page report on technology in education. Tell all the groups that they can use whatever resources they want. The group without computers and those without Internet access can use technology, but they must go and find what they need outside the classroom.
	Upon completion of the assignment, bring the class together, but leave them in their three groups. Have each group share their experience with the assignment. Was it more difficult without a computer or Internet access? How did they cope with the absence of technology? What did they need to do?
	After completing the activity, have students brainstorm how they could help those who do not have technology access. What could the school or community do? Have students think about how education might be different if everyone had equal access to technology.
EXTENSION IDEA	Collect statistics from your classroom about access to technology outside school.
TEACHING TIPS	After students discuss access to technology, have them come up with a list of other things that are needed to make effective use of it (e.g., training, adult support).
	Discuss why some parents may not want digital technology in their homes.
	Discuss options for students who need to use technology to complete assignments outside school.

School Environment and Student Behavior

Guided lessons 7–10 address digital citizenship in terms of rights and responsibilities, etiquette, and security.

GUIDED LESSON 7 • Cyberbullying (Rights and Responsibilities)

NETS ADDRESSED	NETS•T 4.a; NETS•S 5.a
FOCUS QUESTION	What is cyberbullying?
RELATED QUESTIONS	How can students protect themselves while online?
	What should parents know about cyberbullying?
OBJECTIVE	To make students more aware of the issues and consequences of cyberbullying.
RESOURCES NEEDED	Cyberbullying: Always On? Always Aware!: www.cyberbullying.org www.cyberbullying.ca
	Bully OnLine—Cyberbullying on the Internet: www.bullyonline.org/related/cyber.htm
ACTIVITY DESCRIPTION	Ask students if they have heard the term cyberbullying. If they have, do they know what it is and what it involves? If not, provide a definition (see Resources Needed, above) and provide examples (e.g., saying derogatory things, making threats, or ridiculing others using email or blogs).
	Ask students if this has happened to anyone in the class (be careful—this might be happening), and, if so, how the individuals involved responded to it.
	Ask students to consider what they should do if they are bullied in this way. Brainstorm effective approaches as a group. Explain the consequences for those using these methods of intimidation.
EXTENSION IDEA	Find statistics on cyberbullying (e.g., www.cyberbullying.us or www.isafe.org) and provide them to the administration. Suggest that the information be provided to parents in the school newsletter or website.
TEACHING TIPS	Provide resources to students so they know what to do if they are bullied online or through other digital means.
	Provide information to parents so they can understand technology issues such as cyberbullying.
	Understand that some students may have been harassed in this way. Make sure resources are made available to help those who are having problems.

Realize that, by providing information about cyberbullying, you might unwittingly give students some ideas on how to do it to others. Remind students that their actions are never anonymous on the Internet—there are many ways to discover a user's true identity and track the sites they visit.

GUIDED LESSON 8 • Digital Plagiarism (Rights and Responsibilities)

NETS ADDRESSED   NETS•T 4.a; NETS•S 5.a

FOCUS QUESTION   What do students need to know about digital plagiarism?

RELATED QUESTIONS   How can teachers help students understand the issues of digital plagiarism?

How can schools encourage students to use the Internet for research and appropriately document their sources of information?

OBJECTIVE   To make students more aware of the issues related to misrepresenting other peoples' material as their own (plagiarism).

RESOURCES NEEDED   Plagiarism Stoppers: A Teachers Guide: www.ncusd203.org/central/html/where/plagiarism_stoppers.html

Plagiarism.org: www.plagiarism.org

ACTIVITY DESCRIPTION   Provide students with a definition of plagiarism and discuss how it concerns them. Explain that other writers' ideas can be used in their papers, but they need to be cited correctly.

As a class, perform a sample Internet research activity and show students how to collect and cite information from the web (see Citation Resources sidebar).

Explain to students that there are several ways to tell if material has been plagiarized. Let them know that if their work does not appear to be their own, it will be investigated.

Provide support to students beginning the process of writing and citing sources they find on the Internet.

EXTENSION IDEAS   Inform other teachers in the school what students have learned about the proper citation of Internet resources. Have teachers keep an eye out for signs of digital plagiarism.

TEACHING TIPS   Inform students that many resources on plagiarism are available (both on the Internet and in print), and emphasize that ignorance is not a justifiable defense for plagiarism; all references must be cited correctly.

Provide opportunities for learning proper citation methods before requiring it in a research paper. Teach students about the consequences of passing off other people's material as their own. Make sure that your school or district has an official plagiarism policy.

Talk to the administration about handling digital plagiarism. Have this discussion before it becomes an issue.

Citation Resources

Students looking for information on citing materials correctly can visit websites such as these:

Citation Machine:
    http://citationmachine.net

Knight Cite:
    http://calvin.edu/library/knightcite/

Noodle Tools:
    www.noodletools.com

GUIDED LESSON 9 • Digital Etiquette When Working Online (Etiquette)

NETS ADDRESSED	NETS•T 4.c; NETS•S 5.d
FOCUS QUESTION	What etiquette should be used while working online?
RELATED QUESTIONS	Do students need to follow rules when working online?
	How do students know what behavior is appropriate online?
OBJECTIVE	To make students more aware of appropriate online etiquette.
RESOURCES NEEDED	Life 123—Texting Etiquette: www.life123.com/holidays/etiquette/texting/text-messaging.shtml
	Netiquette Home Page: www.albion.com/netiquette/
ACTIVITY DESCRIPTION	Divide students into groups of three or four. Ask each group to come up with five rules to follow when working online.
	Compile a list from the rules created by each group. Discuss the activity with the class and determine whether other rules may be important to include.
EXTENSION IDEA	Collect all the rules from each of the groups. Create a quiz at the end of the lesson on etiquette and see how well the students remember what has been discussed.
TEACHING TIPS	Reinforce with the students that good digital etiquette is important for everyone who uses digital technology. Everyone must be made aware that an individual's use of technology may affect others.
	Emphasize that good digital etiquette benefits everyone, which is the goal of digital citizenship.
	Provide support for students who do not see the need for policies or rules. Show that without these policies it would be difficult for large numbers of users to work together online.

GUIDED LESSON 10 • Protecting the School's Network (Security)

NETS ADDRESSED NETS•T 4.a; NETS•S 5.a

FOCUS QUESTION What should students do to help keep the school's technology resources secure?

RELATED QUESTIONS How can schools protect their network from intrusion?

What user behaviors pose a threat to network security?

OBJECTIVE To make students aware that their school's network needs to be protected from outside threats.

RESOURCE NEEDED PC World—Tips and Tweaks: Safeguard Your Valuables: www.pcworld.com/article/123471/tips_and_tweaks_safeguard_your_valuables.html

ACTIVITY DESCRIPTION Discuss ways that computer hardware and software can be damaged from internal and external threats (e.g., viruses, corrupt hard disks, spyware). With students, create a list of threats.

Once a list has been completed, discuss how to protect the technology from these threats. What changes must be made to the technology (or how it is used) to help protect it from these threats?

Have students determine which (if any) of these prevention costs and procedural changes outweigh the possible threats.

EXTENSION IDEA Have students interview business owners to see how they protect their hardware and networks, and what employees do to help these efforts.

TEACHING TIPS Have technology leaders in the school or district come into the classroom and discuss policies that protect the network and students. Have students ask what might happen if these policies were not in place.

Discuss with students any security measures they have at home. Have students talk to their parents about additional steps they could take.

Help students understand the reasoning behind certain rules and "locked down" computers. Work with students to see the cost-benefit of prevention measures such as antivirus, spyware, and antispam software.

Student Life Outside the School Environment

Guided lessons 11–15 address digital citizenship in terms of commerce, health and wellness, and law.

GUIDED LESSON 11 • Purchasing Items Online (Commerce)

NETS ADDRESSED	NETS•T 4.a; NETS•S 5.a, 5.c
FOCUS QUESTION	What do students need to know about researching and purchasing items online?
RELATED QUESTIONS	What types of online purchases are safe and secure, and what types are not?
	How can parents be involved in students' online purchases?
OBJECTIVE	To help students understand how to make appropriate decisions when purchasing items online.
RESOURCE NEEDED	Microsoft Home Magazine—Tips for Teens Who Shop Online: www.microsoft.com/canada/home/safety-and-security/articles/tips-for-teens-who-shop-online.aspx
ACTIVITY DESCRIPTION	Provide students with some basic shopping strategies for researching and purchasing items online. Review the use of general search engines such as Google, Yahoo, or Bing, as well as commerce-specific search engines such as Bizrate, Dealtime, and Froogle. Do actual searches for items online and review the process with several sites. Identify some specific items that may be sold by only one retailer.
	Emphasize that purchasing items online requires looking for secure sites—ones that encrypt and protect your personal information. Have them look for clues regarding the security of a site, such as the lock symbol at the bottom of the web browser's bar. Also have students look for specific statements of security on a given website. Go through the process of purchasing an item, as well as purchasing a song from a music website.
EXTENSION IDEA	Have students talk to their parents about online purchasing. If their parents buy online, have them share ideas about appropriate purchasing methods and strategies.
TEACHING TIPS	Reiterate to students that they need to consult with their parents when making purchases online.
	Provide resources on all aspects of the search and purchase process so students can understand the importance of good decision making.
	Inform parents that you are providing information about the process, but are advocating that students talk to parents before making purchases online.

Explain how to make appropriate decisions with various types of commercial sites—buying music from iTunes (or similar sites); buying or selling on an auction site such as eBay; or buying "virtual" merchandise for online games. Be sure to survey student attitudes on these various commercial transactions.

GUIDED LESSON 12 • Buying and Selling on Auction Sites (Commerce)

NETS ADDRESSED	NETS•T 4.a; NETS•S 5.a, 5.c
FOCUS QUESTION	What should students know about buying and selling items on online auction sites?
RELATED QUESTIONS	How can students safely learn how to buy and sell items from online auction sites such as eBay?
	How can students determine which online auction sites are safe for buying and selling?
OBJECTIVE	To determine the precautions that need to be taken when buying or selling items on online auction sites.
RESOURCES NEEDED	eBay Buying Tips: http://pages.ebay.com/help/buy/tips.html
	eBay Selling Tips: http://pages.ebay.com/help/sell/seller-tips.html
	Online Shopping: www.onguardonline.gov/topics/online-shopping.aspx
ACTIVITY DESCRIPTION	Survey students on whether they have bought or sold items through online auction sites. Have students come up with a list of dos and don'ts when purchasing items on such sites. Have students rank the items from most important to least important.
	Discuss why it is important to have some knowledge before buying and selling items on auction sites.
EXTENSION IDEA	Have students who have purchased items online explain how they learned to find and purchase them. Ask where they learned the process (e.g., on their own, from parents, from friends)?
TEACHING TIPS	Provide students with background information on the issues that can arise with buying and selling online (see Digital Security).
	Provide information on how to identify appropriate online auction sites for buying and selling items. Make sure that students look for these identifiers when they are online.

Inform parents that there will be a discussion about online selling and buying. Make sure they know that the intent of the lesson is not to encourage students to buy or sell items online, but to make them better consumers.

Have students share information from the lesson with their parents. Check with parents to make sure they have no misunderstandings about the lesson or its objective.

GUIDED LESSON 13 • How Do You Spend Your Free Time? (Health and Wellness)

NETS ADDRESSED NETS•T 4.a, 4.c; NETS•S 5.a

FOCUS QUESTION Do students spend too much time using digital technologies?

RELATED QUESTIONS Why should students be concerned with overuse of digital technologies?

How much do peers influence the use of certain technologies?

OBJECTIVE To illustrate how much time students use technology.

RESOURCES NEEDED Kaiser Family Foundation—
Generation M: Media in the Lives of 8–18 Year-olds:
www.kff.org/entmedia/entmedia030905pkg.cfm

TechNewsWorld—Personal Tech Addiction:
www.technewsworld.com/story/53102.html

ACTIVITY DESCRIPTION Create a questionnaire on students' use of technology, breaking it into sections for "at school," "at home," and "other." Make sure to list items such as surfing the Internet, using an MP3 player, and talking on a cell phone. For best results, have students complete this survey anonymously.

Alternatively, have students keep a record of their technology use for one week. They should record specifically what they were doing, what they were feeling, where they were, the length of time technology was used, and any other criteria you deem important.

Compile the information gathered by students and see where and how much they are using technology on a daily basis.

Ask students where they learn most about technology. Do they think about how they are using the technology with respect to others?

EXTENSION IDEA Take the information gathered from the students and determine the kinds of technology they are using. Have students identify the technologies they might use more often if they were more widely available in school.

TEACHING TIPS

Ask students to think about their technology use. Have them discuss how the use of technology makes them feel.

Compare the results gathered in your classroom with national averages (see Resources Needed). Are your students following the national trends?

Help students look beyond the basic uses of technology. Urge them to think about all uses of technology (game players, cell phones, MP3 players, etc.).

Reiterate that technology use is never wrong in and of itself. Rather, how technology is used (and how often) determines appropriateness.

GUIDED LESSON 14 • Computer Ergonomics (Health and Wellness)

NETS ADDRESSED

NETS•T 4.b; NETS•S 5.c

FOCUS QUESTION

What is ergonomics and what does it have to do with technology?

RELATED QUESTIONS

Can using computers be harmful to students over time?

What should be done to decrease repetitive stress injuries?

OBJECTIVE

To make students more aware of the physical issues related to technology use.

RESOURCES NEEDED

IBM—Healthy Computing:
www.pc.ibm.com/ww/healthycomputing/

Safe Computing Tips:
www.safecomputingtips.com

ACTIVITY DESCRIPTION

Spend some time discussing ergonomics and its effect on technology use.

Have students study their school and document where technology is used. Have them determine whether the principles of good ergonomics are being adequately considered in all locations.

Compile a list of ergonomic issues from around the school and provide remedies for these issues.

Invite a school or district technology leader to come and talk about the ergonomic issues that students have identified.

EXTENSION IDEA

Have students look in their own homes for ergonomic issues and talk with their parents about solutions to any issues they find.

TEACHING TIPS

Spend time at the beginning of the lesson discussing good ergonomics and the effects that poor ergonomics can have on a person's health.

Find statistics on carpal tunnel disorders and other repetitive stress problems (see Resources Needed). Show the effects that years of technology use can have on users later in life.

Emphasize to students that some ergonomic issues may be more difficult to solve because of financial or facility constraints. See if students can come up with other ways to solve the problem that don't involve purchasing new items.

GUIDED LESSON 15 • File Sharing (Law)

NETS ADDRESSED	NETS•T 4.a; NETS•S 5.a
FOCUS QUESTION	What is file sharing, and when is it legal or illegal?
RELATED QUESTIONS	Is file sharing always legal or always illegal?
	How do students know what can be downloaded legally and what cannot?
OBJECTIVE	To make students more aware of the issues surrounding file sharing.
RESOURCES NEEDED	Center for Intellectual Property: www.umuc.edu/cip
	RIAA—Piracy: Online and On the Street: www.riaa.com/physicalpiracy. php?content_selector=piracy_online_the_law
ACTIVITY DESCRIPTION	Divide the class into two groups. One group will argue in support of file sharing and the other will argue against it. Provide time for students to research each side of the argument. Make sure they have concrete examples of legal and illegal file sharing to use in their arguments.
	Have each group designate one or two spokespeople to debate the issue. Hold a debate. After completing the debate, have the class determine which side made a better case. Spend time after the debate discussing the issues raised by both groups.
EXTENSION IDEA	Have students contact lawyers who specialize in digital law and ask them to provide legal arguments for both sides.
TEACHING TIPS	Provide equal time for each group to make its case. Set a limit on the amount of time each group gets. Emphasize that the presentations should be clear and to the point.
	Provide direction for each group. Each group needs to have research to back up the ideas (not just opinions).
	Explain that each group needs to fully support its position. Even if members believe in the other side of the argument, they need to be committed to their position.

Scoring Rubric for Guided Lessons

Use this scoring rubric to assess student comprehension of the topics presented.

OBJECTIVES	Exemplary Performance 4	At or Above Average 3	At or Below Average 2	Low Performance 1	Points Earned
Student has an understanding of the importance of the concept.	Student has a complete grasp of the concept.	Student is not sure about the importance of the concept.	Student is unaware of the importance of the concept.	Student does not understand the topic.	
Student is involved in the classroom activity.	Student is completely engaged.	Student is interested but not engaged.	Student is not providing effort in class.	Student is not interested in the topic.	
Student understands the relevance of the topic to the larger discussion of digital citizenship.	Student has a good grasp of both the topic and digital citizenship.	Student is aware of digital citizenship but unsure of the connection.	Student has only a minimal understanding of either the topic or digital citizenship.	Student does not understand either the topic or digital citizenship.	
Student can come up with related examples of topics within digital citizenship.	Student is able to use information from the activity to come up with new concepts related to digital citizenship.	Student can provide limited examples with prompting from the teacher or other students.	Student has difficulty making the connection between the activity and other examples.	Student is not able to come up with any examples beyond what is presented in the activity.	
Student understands the need to use technology appropriately.	Student makes the connection between appropriate technology use and good citizenship.	Student understands that technology should be used appropriately but believes that some misuse is okay.	Student is having difficulty realizing how inappropriate technology use affects others.	Student cannot understand the need for using technology appropriately.	
At the conclusion of the activity, did the student seem to gain any new ideas or concepts?	Yes, the student seemed to learn many new ideas.	Yes, the student took away some ideas.	Not sure.	No, the student seemed disinterested in the topic.	
Overall, what effort did the student put forth in this activity?	The student has given much effort to the topic.	The student worked hard, but not 100%.	The student did very little during this activity.	The student provided no effort in doing this activity.	
				TOTAL SCORE:	

Holistic Score. The holistic score provides a general level of understanding of the topic and digital citizenship. Look at the holistic score and the description of that score below.

25–28 Exemplary understanding of the topic and digital citizenship. Student has a good understanding of the concept.

22–24 Above average understanding of the topic and digital citizenship. Student understands the topic but still needs additional resources.

20–21 Average understanding of the topic and digital citizenship. Student needs more time to learn about this topic and the overall concept of digital citizenship.

17–19 Low understanding of the topic and digital citizenship. Student has little knowledge of the topic; more work is needed.

Below 17 Student has no understanding of the topic or is uninterested.

Conclusion

This book provides a starting point for administrators, technology leaders, and teachers for thinking about how digital technology should be used in the district as well as in the classroom. But it's only a start. Given the ever-changing nature of digital technology, it would be foolhardy to speculate on what the next technologies will be and how they should be used. Nonetheless, and no matter what new technologies come along, digital citizenship will provide educators with a framework for exploring these technologies with their students.

Digital citizenship is important to other areas of society beyond education (Figure C.1). Educating parents about digital citizenship provides a consistent message to students. Businesses and industries benefit when new employees come into the workforce already fluent in the appropriate use of technology. It is critical for educators to take the lead in this issue. Without such education, our students will find it much more difficult to become productive digital citizens, and our society will be diminished for it.

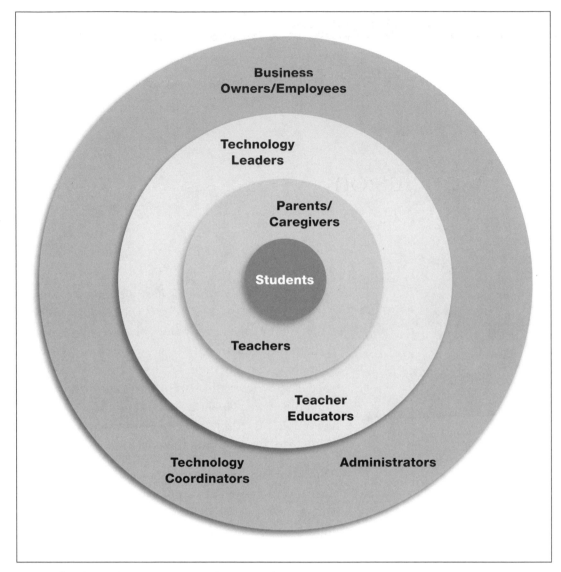

Figure C.1 Target for teaching digital citizenship.

Digital Citizenship and Parents

Because parents are the primary educators of their own children, they too need to be involved in the process of understanding digital citizenship. Many issues addressed in this book (as well as others) need to be exercised in the home. Although there is much good information in this book that parents can use, the issues and scenarios presented here focus on the needs of technology leaders and teachers in the schools. I've also written a book specifically for parents, *Raising a Digital Child* (published under ISTE's HomePage Books imprint), which provides additional information for digital citizenship in the home, with parents as the focus. Both books use the same nine elements, which makes them good companions for each other to teach the concepts of digital citizenship both in school and in the home.

Digital Citizenship and the Law

Advances in digital technology have had a great effect on every level of our society. Because the technologies themselves are value-neutral, individual users must decide how best to use them. Sometimes those individual choices have not been to the benefit of society at large. The victims of these choices have not been idle—we now have a wide variety of laws that protect users of digital technologies and their property. Indeed, issues as diverse as copyright infringement and where and when you can talk on a cell phone are now under legal jurisdiction in the digital world.

The expanding issues that affect technology users are becoming more the purview of the legal system. Issues such as the misrepresentation of oneself on social networking sites, which can lead to the harm of others, have made headlines around the world. Even comments made on Twitter and Facebook have become admissible in court. As mentioned in Chapter 2, the sending and receiving of inappropriate photos is leading to legal consequences. Even the mere possession of these sent photos (whether wanted or not) can cause a teenager to be labeled a sex offender for the rest of his or her life.

Respecting the laws related to digital technology is one aspect of digital citizenship, but by no means is it the only one. Although a good digital citizen recognizes that he or she must understand and follow technology use laws and policies, digital citizenship means much more. Good digital citizens understand the social reasons for adhering to such rules. They think critically about what is acceptable and how their actions affect others in society.

The goal of digital citizenship is to create a citizenry with the tools necessary to evaluate digital technology situations and come to reasonable conclusions prior to acting. Digital technology users must evaluate their own technology use in order to be productive members of a digital society. This society may have laws and policies on technology use, but it will be our understanding of these technologies and how we use them that will define our future.

Digital Citizenship and Business

Statistics show that billions of dollars are lost by businesses each year through the inappropriate use of digital technologies. By having a strong digital citizenship program in the schools, I believe that some of these problems can be mitigated.

When asked what they think the goal of education is, many teachers respond that it is to prepare students to become adults who are "educated, contributing members of society." If technology and its appropriate use is becoming a necessity in the workplace, then shouldn't learning the skills of digital citizenship be a requirement for all students? Educators should use the concept of digital citizenship to prepare students to be efficient, hard-working adults. By having students prepared to be more effective workers using technology, they will be better equipped to compete in the global marketplace.

The Future Is Now

Teachers and technology leaders need a roadmap for the digital future. With history as a guide, it is likely that the next few years will bring a number of changes in the technologies we use everyday. Now is the time to start the discussion. Now is the time to look to the future. And now is the time to make a change.

Digital technologies are not going to diminish in scope, nor are they going to fade away until they become some quaint and forgotten fad. Should educators turn their backs and behave as if digital technology does not exist? Or should they embrace these technologies and begin preparing students to become citizens of a digital society?

The choices that educators make today will shape the future for our students as well as for our society.

Lessons Learned Since the First Edition

Since the release of the first edition of this book in 2007, there have been continuous changes in the relationship between education and technology. Schools and districts have come to the realization that just saying "No" to bad technology practices is not enough and is not helping to prepare students. The elements of digital citizenship have not changed but the issues have become more serious. For example, the issue of students viewing pornography has not gone away, but now students are creating their own pornographic images and sharing them with their friends. Some students are leaving a "digital footprint" of themselves that they may not be proud of in the future.

The concern for educators and parents alike is the seeming disconnect between what students are doing with the technology and what they are doing in their schools and homes. The idea of anonymity, I believe, is causing students to act in a way that they would not want to show their grandmother. Even in the few years since the first edition of this book, the technology has become so personal that much of the inappropriate activity can be done from a smartphone. How are educators and parents to get it across to this next generation of students that they might be leaving behind a trail that they will have to deal with in the future?

The problem that most students do not realize (or do not want to admit) is that others will be using this information to evaluate them in the future. Institutions of higher education are going online and using the "digital footprint" to make decisions about students they have never met. After college, businesses are looking at the digital remnants left behind by applicants to determine if they are fit to work for their companies. Even potential teachers are asked to take down their social networking sites before they student-teach. Some may consider this to be an infringement of an individual's rights, but schools and colleges of education see it as a means to protect their students' reputations.

It may appear from the previous paragraphs that there are only negative issues and no hope in sight. However, there are many schools and districts that seem to be "getting it." Many educators are asking the question, "How do we deal with these issues, and how do we help our students?" Many have found the resources in this book to provide a helpful beginning. Others have begun building on the topics and elements of digital citizenship to create their own programs on which they are working with their teachers, parents, and students. These topics and issues are not unique to one country, but can be found around the world. As a matter of fact there are many active users of digital citizenship in numerous countries, from the United States to Qatar, Belgium, Canada, and Australia.

From the beginning of writing this book, I've been concerned with creating a curriculum that dictated exactly what should be covered and when. From the feedback I have received, it appears that this is becoming more and more of a necessity. Schools and districts are finding it far too much work to create these programs on their own. I hope that in the near future a program can be drafted and made available to schools and districts that are interested in using such a curriculum. The concept would be similar in organization to the teaching of civic understanding that many schools use today to explain how and where students fit into the social order: it will begin with those around them and build outward.

Digital citizenship poses a more difficult problem, however, because unlike civics, which offers the organization of cities, states, and countries, in the digital realm every child can begin with access to the entire world. A curriculum of digital citizenship will need to be taught at two levels at once—the horizontal (the world immediately around them) and the vertical (the connection to the rest of the world). These will not be easy concepts to master, but they need to be taught to prepare students to work and compete in a digital world. These concepts will also need to be taught to young students (beginning in first through third grade) so they can begin the process before they learn inappropriate lessons.

There has been much support and interest in digital citizenship from many people around the world since we published the first edition. It is becoming apparent that more and more people are seeing the importance of teaching and learning these skills for a lifetime. I hope that the work of these pioneers will not be overlooked in the years to come.

Definition of Terms

acceptable use policy (AUP). Policy set up by the network administrator or other school leaders in conjunction with their technology needs and safety concerns. This policy restricts the manner in which a network may be used and provides guidelines for teachers using technology in the classroom. (4teachers.org, 2004)

Android platform. Google Inc.'s open and free software stack that includes an operating system, middleware and also key applications for use on mobile devices, including smart-phones. (Webopedia, 2010)

Bing. A search engine from Microsoft. Microsoft calls it a "Decision Engine," because it's designed to return search results in a format that organizes answers to address your needs. (Webopedia, 2010)

BlackBerry. A line of mobile email devices and services from Research In Motion (RIM). BlackBerry is a complete package that includes airtime, software, and choice of Black-Berry mobile device. (Webopedia, 2010)

blog (from *web log*). A website that contains dated text entries in reverse chronological order about a topic (most recent entry first). Blogs serve many purposes, from personal journals to online newsletters to "ranting and raving." Written by one person or a group of contributors, entries contain commentary, observations, and opinions, and may include images, audio, video, links to other sites and even a search facility for finding earlier entries. (TechWeb, 2011)

browser. Short for *web browser*, a software application used to locate and display web pages. The two most popular browsers are Microsoft Internet Explorer and Firefox. Both of these are *graphical browsers*, which means that they can display graphics as well as text. In addition, most modern browsers can present multimedia information, including sound and video, though they require plug-ins for some formats. (Webopedia, 2010)

cell phone (mobile telephone or **cellular telephone).** Cellular telephone, sometimes called mobile telephone, is a type of short-wave analog or digital telecommunication [service] in which a subscriber has a wireless connection from a mobile telephone to a relatively nearby transmitter. The transmitter's span of coverage is called a cell. (WhatIs.com, 1998)

citizen. Person who works against injustice, not for individual recognition or personal advantage, but for the benefit of all people. In realizing this task—shattering privileges, ensuring information and competence, acting in favor of all—each person becomes a citizen. (Johnson & Nissenbaum, 1995)

cloud computing. General term for anything that involves delivering hosted services over the Internet. ...The name *cloud computing* was inspired by the cloud symbol that's often used to represent the Internet in flow charts and diagrams. A cloud service has three distinct characteristics that differentiate it from traditional hosting. It is [free, as with Google apps and many blogs, or] sold on demand, typically by the minute or the hour; it is elastic—a user can have as much or as little of a service as they want at any given time; and the service is fully managed by the provider (the consumer needs nothing but a personal computer and Internet access). (WhatIs.com, 2007)

computer ethics. "Analysis of the nature and social impact of computer technology and the corresponding formulation and justification of policies for the ethical use of such technology." (Johnson & Nissenbaum, 1995)

computer literacy. Level of expertise and familiarity someone has with computers. Computer literacy generally refers to the ability to use applications rather than to program. Individuals who are very computer literate are sometimes called power users. (PC Webopedia, 2004)

cyberspace. Metaphor for describing the nonphysical terrain created by computer systems. Online systems, for example, create a cyberspace within which people can communicate with one another (by email), do research, or simply window shop. Like physical space, cyberspace contains objects (files, mail messages, graphics, etc.) and different modes of transportation and delivery. Unlike real space, though, exploring cyberspace does not require any physical movement other than pressing keys on a keyboard or moving a mouse. The term was coined by author William Gibson in his 1984 sci-fi novel *Neuromancer.* (PC Webopedia, 2004)

digital divide (or digital dirt road divide). Discrepancy between people who have access to and the resources to use new information and communication tools, such as the Internet, and people who do not have the resources and access to the technology. The term also describes the discrepancy between those who have the skills, knowledge, and abilities to use the technologies and those who do not. The digital divide can exist between those living in rural areas and those living in urban areas, between the educated and uneducated, between economic classes, and on a global scale between more and less industrially developed nations. (PC Webopedia, 2004)

distance learning. Type of education, typically college-level, in which students work on their own at home or at the office and communicate with faculty and other students through email, electronic forums, videoconferencing, chat rooms, bulletin boards, instant messaging, and other forms of computer-based communication. Most distance learning programs include a computer-based training (CBT) system and communications tools to produce a virtual classroom. Because the Internet and World Wide Web are accessible from virtually all computer platforms, they serve as the foundation for many distance learning systems. (PC Webopedia, 2004)

download. To save a file onto your computer from another source, like the Internet. People often download files, such as freeware, shareware, installation software, sounds, movie clips, text files, or news streams, onto their computer for viewing or listening. (4teachers.org, 2004)

e-commerce (electronic commerce or EC). EC is the buying and selling of goods and services on the Internet, especially the World Wide Web. (WhatIs.com, 2000)

email (electronic mail). Transmission of messages over communications networks. … Most mainframes, minicomputers, and computer networks have an email system. (PC Webopedia, 2004)

ergonomics. The science of fitting the workplace to the worker. Ergonomics involves reducing exposure to physical trauma, redesigning tools and workstations, and preventing and treating cumulative trauma disorders (CTDs), such as carpal tunnel syndrome and tendonitis. (Occupational and Environmental Health Center, 2004)

Facebook. The name of a social networking site (SNS) that connects people with friends and others who work, study, and live around them. People use Facebook to keep in touch with friends, post photos, share links, and exchange other information. Facebook users can see only the profiles of confirmed friends and the people in their networks. (Webopedia, 2010)

firewall. Hardware and/or software that separates a local area network (LAN) into two or more parts for security purposes. (4teachers.org, 2004)

Google. Refers to both the company, Google, and the Internet search engine it developed. It is the largest public Internet search engine, in terms of indexed content and number of users. Google also offers content-specific searches for Blogs, Books, Video, Images, Maps, Local, Mobile, and country-specific searches. Google, the corporation, also provides a large number of Internet (cloud)-based services and applications including blogging, mapping, shopping, research, office productivity, and more. (Webopedia, 2010)

handheld computer. Handheld device that combines computing, telephone/fax, Internet, and networking features. A typical handheld computer can function as a cellular phone, fax sender, web browser, and personal organizer. Unlike portable computers, most handheld computers began as pen-based, using a stylus rather than a keyboard for input. (PC Webopedia, 2004)

home page. Page on the Internet that most often gives users access to the rest of the website. A site is a collection of pages. (4teachers.org, 2004)

hotspot. (Sometimes called a Wi-Fi hotspot.) Specific geographic location in which an access point provides public wireless broadband network services to mobile visitors through a WLAN (wireless local area network). Hotspots are often located in heavily populated places such as airports, train stations, libraries, marinas, convention centers, and hotels. Hotspots typically have a short range of access. (PC Webopedia, 2004)

information literacy. Ability to locate, evaluate, and use information to become independent lifelong learners. (Southern Association of Colleges and Schools, 1996)

instant messaging (IM). Exchanging messages in real time between two or more people. Unlike a dial-up system such as the telephone, instant messaging requires that both parties be logged on to their IM service at the same time. Also known as a "chatting," IM has become very popular for both business and personal use. In business, IM provides a way to contact co-workers at any time of the day, providing that they are at their computers. Because you are signaled when other IM users have logged on, you know they are back at their desks, at least for the moment. Thus, IM is often used as a way to avoid telephone tag, whether the communication continues as text messages or winds up as a traditional phone call. (TechWeb, 2004)

Internet. Global network connecting millions of computers. [Hundreds of] countries are linked into exchanges of data, news, and opinions. (PC Webopedia, 2004)

iPad. A new handheld computing device launched by Apple Inc. in January 2010. The iPad is designed for consumers who want a mobile device that is bigger than a smartphone but smaller than a laptop for entertainment multimedia. (Webopedia, 2010)

iPhone. An Internet-enabled smartphone developed by Apple. The iPhone combines mobile phone capabilities with a wireless Internet device, and an iPod into one product. The iPhone also includes a 3.5-inch multi-touch screen, rather than a keyboard, that can be manipulated by users with two finger touches. (Webopedia, 2010)

iPod. Apple's iPod is a small portable MP3 music player [and video player and photo storage device]. Users can transfer songs [videos, games, and photos] to their iPod with their computer, iTunes, and the iPod software. (PC Webopedia, 2005)

ISP (Internet service provider). Pronounced as separate letters. For a fee or free, an ISP company provides both personal and business access to the Internet.

IT (information technology). Pronounced as separate letters, IT refers to the broad subject concerned with all aspects of managing and processing information, especially within a large organization or company. Because computers are central to information management, computer departments within companies and universities are often called IT departments. Some companies refer to this department as IS (information services) or MIS (management information services). (PC Webopedia, 2004)

microblog. A type of blog that lets users publish short text updates. Bloggers can usually use a number of services for the updates including instant messaging, email, or Twitter. The posts are called microposts, while the act of using these services to update your blog is called microblogging. Social networking sites, such as Facebook, also use a microblogging feature in user profiles called "Status Updates." (Webopedia, 2010)

mobile phone. See cell phone.

MP3. File extension for MPEG, audio layer 3. Layer 3 is one of three coding schemes (layer 1, layer 2, and layer 3) for the compression of audio signals. Because MP3 files are small, they can easily be transferred across the Internet. Controversy arises when copyrighted songs are sold and distributed illegally from websites. (PC Webopedia, 2004)

MP4. A graphics and video standard that is based on MPEG-1 and MPEG-2 and Apple QuickTime technology. MPEG-4 files are smaller than JPEG or QuickTime files, so they are designed to transmit video and images over a narrower bandwidth and can mix video with text, graphics, and 2-D and 3-D animation layers. (Webopedia, 2010)

multitasking. The concurrent performance of several jobs by a computer. Also, the performance of multiple tasks at one time. (Merriam-Webster, 2011)

netbook. A small portable computing device, similar to a notebook. …What typically differentiates a netbook from a notebook is its physical size, price, and computing power. (Webopedia, 2010)

netiquette. A neologism based on "Internet etiquette." These are etiquette guidelines for posting messages to online services, and particularly Internet newsgroups. Netiquette covers not only rules to maintain civility in discussions (i.e., avoiding flames), but also special guidelines unique to the electronic nature of forum messages. For example, netiquette advises the use of simple formats because complex formatting may not appear correctly for all readers. In most cases, netiquette is enforced by fellow users who will vociferously object if you break a rule of netiquette. (PC Webopedia, 2004)

phishing. Pronounced "fishing." A scam designed to steal valuable information such as credit cards, social security numbers, user IDs, and passwords. Also known as "brand spoofing." An official-looking email is sent to potential victims pretending to be from their ISP, retail store, or some other authorized group, claiming that because of internal accounting errors or some other pretext, certain information must be updated to continue the service. (TechWeb, 2004)

plagiarize. To steal and pass off (the ideas or words of another) as one's own; [to] use (another's production) without crediting the source; to commit literary theft; [to] present as new and original an idea or product derived from an existing source. (Merriam-Webster, 2011)

podcasting. Similar in nature to RSS, which allows users to subscribe to a set of feeds to view syndicated Website content. With podcasting, however, you have a set of subscriptions that are checked regularly for updates and instead of reading the feeds on your computer screen, you listen to the new content on your iPod (or like device). (PC Webopedia, 2005)

search engine. Any of a number of giant databases on the Internet that store data on websites and their corresponding URLs. Some popular search engines are Google, Yahoo!, Bing, Metacrawler, Alta Vista, and Excite. (4teachers.org, 2004)

smartphone. A cell phone that includes additional software functions (as email or Internet browser). (Merriam-Webster, 2011)

RSS. RSS [rich site summary or really simple syndication] is the acronym used to describe the de facto standard for the *syndication of web content*. RSS is an XML-based format and while it can be used in different ways for content distribution, its most widespread usage is in distributing news headlines on the web. (Webopedia, 2010)

sexting. Sexting refers to an act of sending sexually explicit materials through mobile phones. The word is derived from the combination of two terms, sex and texting. (US Legal: http://definitions.uslegal.com/s/sexting/)

social network. An association of people drawn together by family, work, or hobby. The term was first coined by professor J. A. Barnes in the 1950s, who defined the size of a social network as a group of about 100 to 150 people. On the web, social networking sites such as MySpace, Facebook, and Twitter have expanded the concept to include a company's customers, a celebrity's fans, and a politician's constituents. (PCMag.com—Encyclopedia, 2011)

technology integration. Planned, systematic introduction and institutionalization of technology into schools and organizations. (Pownell, 2002)

text messaging. Sending short text messages to a device such as a cellular phone, handheld computer, or pager. Text messaging is used for messages that are no longer than a few hundred characters. The term is usually applied to messaging that takes place between two or more mobile devices. (PC Webopedia, 2004)

3G. An International Telecommunications Union specification for the third generation (analog cellular was the first generation, digital PCS the second) of mobile communications. (Webopedia, 2010)

Twitter. A free social messaging tool that lets people stay connected through brief text message updates up to 140 characters in length [tweets]. Twitter is based on you answering the question "What are you doing?" You then post thoughts, observations, and goings-on during the day. Your update is posted on your Twitter profile page through SMS text messaging, the Twitter website, instant messaging, RSS, email, or through other social applications and sites, such as Facebook. (Webopedia, 2010)

URL (uniform resource locators). Address of any given site on the Internet. (4teachers.org, 2004)

virtual. Not real. The term virtual is popular among computer scientists and is used in a wide variety of situations. In general, it distinguishes something that is merely conceptual from something that has physical reality. For example, virtual memory refers to an imaginary set of locations, or addresses, where data can be stored. It is imaginary in the sense that the memory area is not the same as the real physical memory composed of transistors. The difference is a bit like the difference between an architect's plans for a house and the actual house. A computer scientist might call the plans a virtual house. Another analogy is the difference between the brain and the mind. The mind is a virtual brain. It exists conceptually, but the actual physical matter is the brain. (PC Webopedia, 2004)

Web 2.0. The term given to describe a second generation of the World Wide Web that is focused on the ability for people to collaborate and share information online. Web 2.0 basically refers to the transition from static HTML web pages to a more dynamic web that is more organized and is based on serving web applications to users. Other improved functionality of Web 2.0 includes open communication with an emphasis on web-based communities of users, and more open sharing of information. (Webopedia, 2010)

web browser. See browser.

Wi-Fi (wireless fidelity). The generic term for any type of network that specifies an over-the-air interface between a wireless client and a base station or between two wireless clients. The Wi-Fi Alliance expanded the generic use of the term in an attempt to stop confusion about wireless LAN interoperability. (PC Webopedia, 2004)

Wi-Fi hotspot. See hotspot.

wiki. A collaborative website comprises the perpetual collective work of many authors. Similar to a blog in structure and logic, a wiki allows anyone to edit, delete, or modify content that has been placed on the website using a browser interface, including the work of previous authors. In contrast, a blog, typically authored by an individual, does not allow visitors to change the original posted material, only add comments to the original content. The term wiki refers to either the website or the software used to create the site. Wiki wiki means "quick" in Hawaiian. (Webopedia, 2010)

wireless. Telecommunications in which electromagnetic waves (rather than some form of wire) carry the signal over part or all of the communication path. (WhatIs.com, 2000)

All definitions from the Tech-along Technology Glossary at 4teachers.org are © 1995–2006 ALTEC, the University of Kansas. Reprinted with permission. http://4teachers.org/ techalong/glossary

All definitions from Merriam-Webster are © 2011Merriam-Webster Inc. Reprinted with permission from the Merriam-Webster Online Dictionary (www.merriam-webster.com).

All definitions from Webopedia are © Jupitermedia Corporation. All rights reserved.

APPENDIX **B**

Bibliography

References

Bailey, G. D. (1996). Technology leadership: Ten essential buttons for understanding technology integration in the 21st century. *Educational Considerations, 23*(2), 2–6.

Blanche, T. M. (2004). Wikis. *Collaborative learning environments sourcebook.* Retrieved September 29, 2004, from www.criticalmethods.org/collab/

CyberAtlas. (2003). Study: *Colleges a gateway to software piracy.* Retrieved September 30, 2003 from www.internetnews.com/stats/article.php/3078651

Duncan, A. (2010). *National educational technology plan: Transforming American education: Learning powered by technology.* Washington, DC: U.S. Department of Education, Office of Educational Technology, Government Printing Office. Retrieved from www.ed.gov/technology/netp-2010

Fitzer, K., & Peterson, J. (2002). *Enforcing acceptable use policies.* Retrieved October 17, 2005, from http://ed.uiuc.edu/wp/crime-2002/aup.htm

4teachers.org. (2004). Technology glossary. Retrieved February 22, 2004, from http://4teachers.org

Greenspan, R. (2003). *Cell phone courtesy lacking.* Retrieved November 11, 2003, from www.internetnews.com/stats/article.php/3101231

Gross, D. (2009). *Social networks and kids: How young is too young?* Retrieved on November 16, 2010 from http://articles.cnn.com/2009-11-02/tech/kids.social.networks

Harris Interactive. (2010). *YouthPulse and Youth EquiTrend.* Retrieved from www.harrisinteractive.com

IFPI. (2009). *IFPI digital music report 2009: Key statistics.* Retrieved November 25, 2010, from www.ifpi.org/content/library/DMR2009-key-statistics.pdf

International Ergonomics Association. (2002). *What is ergonomics?* Retrieved March 10, 2004, from www.iea.cc/01_what/What is Ergonomics.html

International Society for Technology in Education (ISTE). (2007). *National educational technology standards for students.* Eugene, OR: Author. Also available online at www.iste.org/standards/nets-for-students.aspx

International Society for Technology in Education (ISTE). (2008). *National educational technology standards for teachers.* Eugene, OR: Author. Also available online at www.iste.org/standards/nets-for-teachers.aspx

International Society for Technology in Education (ISTE). (2009). *National educational technology standards for administrators.* Eugene, OR: Author. Also available online at www.iste.org/standards/nets-for-administrators.aspx

Johnson, D. G., & Nissenbaum, H. (1995; 2006). *Computers, ethics & social values.* Upper Saddle River, NJ: Prentice Hall.

Jupiter Media Matrix. (2001). *Jupiter metrics: Marketing & branding, 2Q 2001.* Retrieved April 17, 2004, from www.jupiterresearch.com/bin/item.pl/research:concept/1215/id=85019

Kentucky Department of Education (2011), Guidelines for Creating Acceptable Use Policies. Retrieved January 10, 2011, from www.education.ky.gov/KDE/Administrative+Resources/Technology/Additional+Technology+Resources

Kinnaman, D. (1995–2006). *Critiquing acceptable use policies.* Retrieved June 27, 2005, from www.prismnet.com/~kinnaman/aupessay

Lenhart, A. (2009). *Teens and sexting.* Retrieved from pewInternet.org/Reports/2009/Teens-and-Sexting.aspx

Lenhart, A., Purcell, K., Smith, A., & Zickuhr, K. (2010). *Social media and young adults.* Retrieved from http://pewInternet.org/Reports/2010/Social-Media-and-Young-Adults.aspx

Lessig, L. (2006). *Code: And other laws of Cyberspace, Version 2.0.* New York, NY: Basic Books. "Codev2" is available online at http://codev2.cc/download+remix/.

Manjoo, F. (2001). *Carpal study stress syndrome?* Retrieved October 15, 2003, from www.wired.com/politics/law/news/2001/06/44400

Mark, R. (2003). *School web access soars, digital divide still remains.* Retrieved November 12, 2003, from www.internetnews.com/ec-news/article.php/3101041

Merriam-Webster. (2011). *Merriam-Webster's online dictionary.* Retrieved from www.merriam-webster.com

McCain, T. & Jukes, I. (2001). *Windows on the future: Education in the age of technology.* Thousand Oaks, CA: Corwin Press.

McGuire, D. (2004, May 18). Report: Kids pirate music freely. *The Washington Post.* Retrieved June 6, 2004, from www.washingtonpost.com/wp-dyn/articles/A37231-2004May18.html

MP3 file. (2006). In *Encyclopedia Britannica Online.* Retrieved September 19, 2006, from www.britannica.com

multitasking. (2011). In *Merriam-Webster's online dictionary.* Retrieved from www.m-w.com/dictionary/multitasking

Occupational and Environmental Health Center. (2004). *Ergonomic Technology Center.* Retrieved September 18, 2006, from www.oehc.uchc.edu/ergo.asp

Paulson, A. (2003, December 30). Internet bullying. The Christian Science Monitor. Retrieved January 5, 2004, from www.csmonitor.com/2003/1230/p11s01-legn.html

PC Webopedia. (2004). Dictionary main page. Retrieved from www.pcwebopedia.com

plagiarize. (2011). In *Merriam-Webster's online dictionary.* Retrieved from www.m-w.com/dictionary/plagiarize

Pownell, D. (2002). Implementing handheld computers in schools: The research, development and validation of a technology leader's resource guide (Doctoral dissertation, Kansas State University, 2002). *Dissertation Abstracts International, 63,* 2515.

Prensky, M. (2001). Digital natives, digital immigrants. *On the Horizon, 9* (5), 10–15.

Selingo, J. (2004, March 18). Hey kid, your backpack is ringing. *The New York Times.* Retrieved from www.nytimes.com/2004/03/18/technology/circuits/18kids.html

sexting. (2010). From US Legal. Retrieved March 25, 2011, from http://definitions.uslegal.com/s/sexting/

Smith, A. (2010a). *Mobile access 2010.* Retrieved from www.pewInternet.com/Reports/2010/Mobile-Access-2010.aspx

Smith, A. (2010b). *Technology trends among people of color.* Center for American Progress Internet Advocacy Roundtable. Retrieved from www.pewInternet.com/Commentary/2010/September/Technology-Trends-Among-People-of-Color.aspx

social network. (2011). In *PCMag.com Encyclopedia.* Retrieved January 30, 2011, from www.pcmag.com/encyclopedia

Southern Association of Colleges and Schools. (1996). *Criteria for accreditation.* Decatur, GA: Commission on Colleges.

Stone, B. (2010). The children of cyberspace: Old fogies by their 20s. *The New York Times.* Retrieved from www.nytimes.com/2010/01/10/weekinreview/10stone.html

TechWeb. (2004, 2011). TechEncyclopedia main page. Retrieved from www.techweb.com/encyclopedia

United States Government Accountability Office. (2006). *Broadband deployment is extensive throughout the United States, but it is difficult to assess the extent of deployment gaps in rural areas.* (GAO-06-426). Washington, DC: U.S. Government Printing Office.

Urbina, I. (2003, October 15). For techies, school bells mean "let the games begin". *The New York Times.* Available from www.nytimes.com

Webopedia. (2010). Dictionary main page. Retrieved from www.webopedia.com

WhatIs.com (1998, 2000, 2007). Dictionary main page. Retrieved from www.whatis.com

Wired News. (2003, May 1). *Students fork it over to RIAA.* Retrieved from www.wired.com/entertainment/music/news/2003/05/58707

Further Reading

Visit the author's website devoted to the topic: **www.digitalcitizenship.net**

Enos, L. (2001). *Report: There's money in teen web surfers.* Retrieved October 15, 2003, from www.ecommercetimes.com/perl/story/12095.html

Greenspan, R. (2003b). *IM challenges corp productivity.* Retrieved September 29, 2003, from www.internetnews.com/stats/article.php/3081031

Greenspan, R. (2003c). *More spending more.* Retrieved October 2, 2003, from www.internetnews.com/stats/article.php/3079601

Greenspan, R. (2003d). *Porn pages reach 260 million.* Retrieved September 29, 2003 from www.internetnews.com/stats/article.php/3083001

Lessig, L. (2001). The future of ideas: The fate of the commons in a connected world (1st ed.). New York, NY: Random House.

Lumley, D., & Bailey, G. (1997). Planning for technology: A guidebook for teachers, technology leaders, and school administrators. Bloomington, IN: National Educational Service.

Pownell, D., & Bailey, G. (2003). Administrative solutions for handheld technology in schools. Eugene, OR: ISTE.

Senge, P. (1990). The fifth discipline: The art and practice of the learning organization. New York, NY: Doubleday.

Zirkel, P.A. (2009). Courtside: All a twitter about sexting. *Kappan, 91*(2) 76–77.

NETS for Students, Teachers, and Administrators

National Educational Technology Standards for Students (NETS•S)

All K–12 students should be prepared to meet the following standards and performance indicators.

1. **Creativity and Innovation**

   Students demonstrate creative thinking, construct knowledge, and develop innovative products and processes using technology. Students:

   a. apply existing knowledge to generate new ideas, products, or processes

   b. create original works as a means of personal or group expression

   c. use models and simulations to explore complex systems and issues

   d. identify trends and forecast possibilities

2. **Communication and Collaboration**

   Students use digital media and environments to communicate and work collaboratively, including at a distance, to support individual learning and contribute to the learning of others. Students:

   a. interact, collaborate, and publish with peers, experts, or others employing a variety of digital environments and media

   b. communicate information and ideas effectively to multiple audiences using a variety of media and formats

   c. develop cultural understanding and global awareness by engaging with learners of other cultures

   d. contribute to project teams to produce original works or solve problems

3. Research and Information Fluency

Students apply digital tools to gather, evaluate, and use information. Students:

    a. plan strategies to guide inquiry

    b. locate, organize, analyze, evaluate, synthesize, and ethically use information from a variety of sources and media

    c. evaluate and select information sources and digital tools based on the appropriateness to specific tasks

    d. process data and report results

4. Critical Thinking, Problem Solving, and Decision Making

Students use critical-thinking skills to plan and conduct research, manage projects, solve problems, and make informed decisions using appropriate digital tools and resources. Students:

    a. identify and define authentic problems and significant questions for investigation

    b. plan and manage activities to develop a solution or complete a project

    c. collect and analyze data to identify solutions and make informed decisions

    d. use multiple processes and diverse perspectives to explore alternative solutions

5. Digital Citizenship

Students understand human, cultural, and societal issues related to technology and practice legal and ethical behavior. Students:

    a. advocate and practice the safe, legal, and responsible use of information and technology

    b. exhibit a positive attitude toward using technology that supports collaboration, learning, and productivity

    c. demonstrate personal responsibility for lifelong learning

    d. exhibit leadership for digital citizenship

6. Technology Operations and Concepts

Students demonstrate a sound understanding of technology concepts, systems, and operations. Students:

    a. understand and use technology systems

    b. select and use applications effectively and productively

    c. troubleshoot systems and applications

    d. transfer current knowledge to the learning of new technologies

National Educational Technology Standards for Teachers (NETS•T)

All classroom teachers should be prepared to meet the following standards and performance indicators.

1. **Facilitate and Inspire Student Learning and Creativity**

   Teachers use their knowledge of subject matter, teaching and learning, and technology to facilitate experiences that advance student learning, creativity, and innovation in both face-to-face and virtual environments. Teachers:

   a. promote, support, and model creative and innovative thinking and inventiveness

   b. engage students in exploring real-world issues and solving authentic problems using digital tools and resources

   c. promote student reflection using collaborative tools to reveal and clarify students' conceptual understanding and thinking, planning, and creative processes

   d. model collaborative knowledge construction by engaging in learning with students, colleagues, and others in face-to-face and virtual environments

2. **Design and Develop Digital-Age Learning Experiences and Assessments**

   Teachers design, develop, and evaluate authentic learning experiences and assessments incorporating contemporary tools and resources to maximize content learning in context and to develop the knowledge, skills, and attitudes identified in the NETS•S. Teachers:

   a. design or adapt relevant learning experiences that incorporate digital tools and resources to promote student learning and creativity

   b. develop technology-enriched learning environments that enable all students to pursue their individual curiosities and become active participants in setting their own educational goals, managing their own learning, and assessing their own progress

   c. customize and personalize learning activities to address students' diverse learning styles, working strategies, and abilities using digital tools and resources

   d. provide students with multiple and varied formative and summative assessments aligned with content and technology standards and use resulting data to inform learning and teaching

3. **Model Digital-Age Work and Learning**

   Teachers exhibit knowledge, skills, and work processes representative of an innovative professional in a global and digital society. Teachers:

  a. demonstrate fluency in technology systems and the transfer of current knowledge to new technologies and situations

  b. collaborate with students, peers, parents, and community members using digital tools and resources to support student success and innovation

  c. communicate relevant information and ideas effectively to students, parents, and peers using a variety of digital-age media and formats

  d. model and facilitate effective use of current and emerging digital tools to locate, analyze, evaluate, and use information resources to support research and learning

4. **Promote and Model Digital Citizenship and Responsibility**

Teachers understand local and global societal issues and responsibilities in an evolving digital culture and exhibit legal and ethical behavior in their professional practices. Teachers:

  a. advocate, model, and teach safe, legal, and ethical use of digital information and technology, including respect for copyright, intellectual property, and the appropriate documentation of sources

  b. address the diverse needs of all learners by using learner-centered strategies and providing equitable access to appropriate digital tools and resources

  c. promote and model digital etiquette and responsible social interactions related to the use of technology and information

  d. develop and model cultural understanding and global awareness by engaging with colleagues and students of other cultures using digital-age communication and collaboration tools

5. **Engage in Professional Growth and Leadership**

Teachers continuously improve their professional practice, model lifelong learning, and exhibit leadership in their school and professional community by promoting and demonstrating the effective use of digital tools and resources. Teachers:

  a. participate in local and global learning communities to explore creative applications of technology to improve student learning

  b. exhibit leadership by demonstrating a vision of technology infusion, participating in shared decision making and community building, and developing the leadership and technology skills of others

  c. evaluate and reflect on current research and professional practice on a regular basis to make effective use of existing and emerging digital tools and resources in support of student learning

  d. contribute to the effectiveness, vitality, and self-renewal of the teaching profession and of their school and community

National Educational Technology Standards for Administrators (NETS•A)

All school administrators should be prepared to meet the following standards and performance indicators.

1. **Visionary Leadership**

   Educational Administrators inspire and lead development and implementation of a shared vision for comprehensive integration of technology to promote excellence and support transformation throughout the organization. Educational Administrators:

   a. inspire and facilitate among all stakeholders a shared vision of purposeful change that maximizes use of digital-age resources to meet and exceed learning goals, support effective instructional practice, and maximize performance of district and school leaders

   b. engage in an ongoing process to develop, implement, and communicate technology-infused strategic plans aligned with a shared vision

   c. advocate on local, state, and national levels for policies, programs, and funding to support implementation of a technology-infused vision and strategic plan

2. **Digital-Age Learning Culture**

   Educational Administrators create, promote, and sustain a dynamic, digital-age learning culture that provides a rigorous, relevant, and engaging education for all students. Educational Administrators:

   a. ensure instructional innovation focused on continuous improvement of digital-age learning

   b. model and promote the frequent and effective use of technology for learning

   c. provide learner-centered environments equipped with technology and learning resources to meet the individual, diverse needs of all learners

   d. ensure effective practice in the study of technology and its infusion across the curriculum

   e. promote and participate in local, national, and global learning communities that stimulate innovation, creativity, and digital-age collaboration

3. **Excellence in Professional Practice**

   Educational Administrators promote an environment of professional learning and innovation that empowers educators to enhance student learning through the infusion of contemporary technologies and digital resources. Educational Administrators:

   a. allocate time, resources, and access to ensure ongoing professional growth in technology fluency and integration

b. facilitate and participate in learning communities that stimulate, nurture, and support administrators, faculty, and staff in the study and use of technology

c. promote and model effective communication and collaboration among stakeholders using digital-age tools

d. stay abreast of educational research and emerging trends regarding effective use of technology and encourage evaluation of new technologies for their potential to improve student learning

4. **Systemic Improvement**

Educational Administrators provide digital-age leadership and management to continuously improve the organization through the effective use of information and technology resources. Educational Administrators:

a. lead purposeful change to maximize the achievement of learning goals through the appropriate use of technology and media-rich resources

b. collaborate to establish metrics, collect and analyze data, interpret results, and share findings to improve staff performance and student learning

c. recruit and retain highly competent personnel who use technology creatively and proficiently to advance academic and operational goals

d. establish and leverage strategic partnerships to support systemic improvement

e. establish and maintain a robust infrastructure for technology including integrated, interoperable technology systems to support management, operations, teaching, and learning

5. **Digital Citizenship**

Educational Administrators model and facilitate understanding of social, ethical, and legal issues and responsibilities related to an evolving digital culture. Educational Administrators:

a. ensure equitable access to appropriate digital tools and resources to meet the needs of all learners

b. promote, model, and establish policies for safe, legal, and ethical use of digital information and technology

c. promote and model responsible social interactions related to the use of technology and information

d. model and facilitate the development of a shared cultural understanding and involvement in global issues through the use of contemporary communication and collaboration tools

Index

A

academic learning. *See* student academic learning and performance

acceptable use policy (AUP)
    adequacy, 12
    defined, 9, 143
    district activity, 74–76
    resources, 13
    review, 86

access, digital
    bridging the digital divide guided lesson, 123
    MP3 files for teaching guided lesson, 121–122
    nine elements framework, 11, 16–19, 44
    providing, outside school activity, 70

Activities
    blogs
        appreciation blog, 61–62
        and wikis for parent communication, 67–68
    buying items online, 79
    communication models, new digital, 63–64
    digital access outside school, providing, 70
    digital citizenship and the district AUP, 74–76
    digital etiquette issues, 73
    digital rights management, 78
    email bingo, 57–59
    personal security, protecting, 77
    technology use
        addiction to, 80
        appropriate, 71
        inappropriate, 72
        in education, 69

    Twitter for gathering information, 65–66
    understanding digital technologies, 60

analysis and feedback, reflection model, 84, 86–87

Android platform, 143

Apple, 146

appreciation blog activity, 61–62

appropriate use
    classroom foundational lessons, 91–94
    Internet guided lesson, 119
    technology activity, 71

auction commerce guided lesson, 130–131

AUP. *See* acceptable use policy (AUP)

awareness in reflection model, 84, 85

B

Bailey, Gerald, 3

behavior. *See* student environment and behavior

Bing (search engine), 143

bingo, email activity, 57–59

Blackberry, 143

blogs
    appreciation blog activity, 61–62
    defined, 62, 143
    new digital communication models activity, 63–64
    for parent communication, activity, 67–68
    primer on, 62

bridging the digital divide guided lesson, 123

browser, 143

bullying in cyberspace guided lesson, 124–125

business use of technology guided lesson, 120

buying items online. *See* commerce

BYOD (bring your own device), 18

C

cellular telephone
    defined, 144
    digital communication, 23
    interruptions guided lesson, 117
    message misinterpretation guided lesson, 118
    role-playing with, 85
chatting, instant messaging (IM), 146
citizen, defined, 7, 144
citizenship, new definition for, 13–14. *See also* digital citizenship
classroom digital citizenship
    Foundational Lessons, 89–114
        appropriate or inappropriate use, 91–94
        digital compass, 95–98
        digital driver's license, 102–111
        lesson format, 90
        NETS, 90
        recognizing the nine elements of digital citizenship, 99–101
        scoring rubric for, 113–114
        what does it mean to be a digital citizen?, 112
    Guided Lessons, 115–135
        lesson format, 116
        school environment and student behavior, 124–128
        scoring rubric, 134–135
        student academic learning and performance, 117–123
        student life outside the school environment, 129–133
    overview, 81–82
    teaching to students, 83–87
        curriculum incorporation, 87
        diagram, 84
        stage 1: awareness, 84, 85
        stage 2: guided practice, 84, 85
        stage 3: modeling and demonstration, 84, 86
        stage 4: feedback and analysis, 84, 86–87
cloud computing, 144
commerce, digital
    auction site buying/selling guided lesson, 130–131
    buying items online activity, 79
    nine elements framework, 11, 20–22, 44
    purchasing items online guided lesson, 129–130
communication
    appreciation blog activity, 61–62

    blogs and wikis for parent communication activity, 67–68
    cell phone interruptions guided lesson, 117
    message misinterpretation guided lesson, 118
    new digital communication models activity, 63–64
    nine elements framework, 11, 23–25, 44
compass classroom foundational lesson, 95–98
computer ergonomics
    defined, 145
    guided lesson, 132–133
computer ethics, 144. *See also* etiquette; rights and responsibilities
computer literacy, 144. *See also* literacy
computing, cloud, 144
cyberbullying guided lesson, 124–125
cyberspace, 144

D

digital access. *See* access
digital citizen, meaning of, classroom foundational lesson, 112
digital citizenship
    audit form, 50–51
    AUP adequacy and resources, 12, 13
    and business, 139
    in the classroom. *See* classroom digital citizenship
    definition, 10
    how to use book, 3–6
    and the law, 139
    lessons learned, 140–141
    new citizenship, 13
    nine elements framework, 15–44
    and parents, 138
    purpose, 12
    reasons for interest in, 1–2, 6, 9–10
    in the school. *See* school digital citizenship
    target for, 138
digital commerce. *See* commerce
digital communication. *See* communication
digital compass classroom foundational lesson, 95–98
digital divide
    bridging guided lesson, 123
    described, 17–18, 144
digital driver's license classroom foundational lesson, 102–111
digital etiquette. *See* etiquette
digital footprint, 23
digital health and wellness. *See* health and wellness

digital law. *See* law

digital literacy. *See* literacy

digital plagiarism guided lesson, 125–126

digital rights and responsibilities.
  See rights and responsibilities

digital security. *See* security

distance learning, 145

district AUP activity, 74–76

download, 145

driver's license classroom foundational
  lesson, 102–111

DRM (digital rights management) activity, 78

E

e-commerce, 145. *See also* commerce

educational standards
  NETS•A, 3, 56, 90, 159–160
  NETS•S, 3, 90, 155–156
  NETS•T, 3, 56, 90, 157–158

email
  bingo activity, 57–59
  defined, 145

environment
  classroom. *See* classroom digital citizenship
  outside school. *See* student life outside the
    school environment
  school. *See* school digital citizenship

ergonomics
  computer ergonomics guided lesson,
    132–133
  defined, 145

ethics, computer, 144. *See also* rights and
  responsibilities

ethnicity and race, digital divide, 17–18

etiquette
  digital issues activity, 73
  netiquette, defined, 147
  nine elements framework, 11, 29–31, 44
  when working online guided lesson, 127

F

Facebook, 139, 145

feedback and analysis, reflection model, 84,
  86–87

file sharing guided lesson, 133

firewall, 145

Foundational Lessons, 89–114
  appropriate vs. inappropriate use, 91–94
  digital compass, 95–98
  digital driver's license, 102–111
  recognizing the nine elements of digital
    citizenship, 99–101

scoring rubric for, 113–114
  what it means to be a digital citizen, 112

framework. *See* models; nine elements
  digital framework

free time choices guided lesson, 131–132

G

Google (company and search engine), 145

graphical browser, 143

Guided Lessons
  appropriate Internet use, 119
  bridging the digital divide, 123
  business use of technology, 120
  buying and selling on auction sites,
    130–131
  cell phone interruptions, 117
  cyberbullying, 124
  computer ergonomics, 132–133
  digital etiquette when working online, 127
  digital plagiarism, 125–126
  file sharing, 133
  free time choices, 131–132
  message misinterpretation, 118
  MP3 files for teaching, 121–122
  protecting the school's network, 128
  purchasing items online, 129–130

guided practice, reflection model, 84, 85

H

handheld computer, 146. *See also* cellular
  telephone, smartphone, netbook

health and wellness
  computer ergonomics guided lesson,
    132–133
  free time choices guided lesson, 131–132
  nine elements framework, 11, 38–40, 44
  technology addiction activity, 80

home page, 146

hotspot, 146

I

IM (instant messaging), 146

inappropriate technology use activity, 72

inappropriate use
  classroom foundational lessons, 91–94
  Internet guided lesson, 119
  technology activity, 71

information literacy, 146. *See also* literacy

information technology (IT), 146–147

instant messaging (IM), 146

intellectual property. *See* law

Internet

    appropriate use guided lesson, 119

    defined, 146

iPad/iPhone/iPod, 146

IT (information technology), 146–147

L

law. *See also* rights and responsibilities

    digital rights management activity, 78

    file sharing guided lesson, 133

    nine elements framework, 11, 31–34, 44

learning. *See* student academic learning
and performance

lessons. *See* Activities; Foundational
Lessons; Guided Lessons

life outside school. *See* student life outside
the school environment

literacy

    appropriate Internet use guided lesson, 119

    business use of technology guided lesson,
120

    computer literacy, 144

    information, 146–147

    new digital communication models activity,
63–64

    nine elements framework, 11, 26–28, 44

    Twitter, information gathering activity,
65–66

    understanding digital technologies activity,
60

    use of technology in education activity, 69

M

manners. *See* etiquette

matching activity, recognizing nine
    elements of digital citizenship, 99–101

message misinterpretation guided lesson, 118

microblog, 147. *See also* Twitter

mobile devices. *See* cellular telephone, smartphone, iPhone

models

    new, for digital communication activity,
63–64

    nine elements digital framework, 15–44

    reflection model, 84, 86

MP3 format

    defined, 147

    players, primer on, 122

    for teaching guided lesson, 121–122

MP4 format, 147

multitasking, 147

N

netbook, 110, 147.

netiquette, 147. *See also* etiquette

NETS•A (National Educational Technology
Standards for Administrators), 3, 56, 90, 159

NETS•S (National Educational Technology
Standards for Students), 3, 90, 155–156

NETS•T (National Educational Technology
Standards for Teachers), 3, 56, 90, 157

network security, guided lesson, 128

new digital communication models activity,
63–64

nine elements digital framework, 15–44. *See also*
additional details under each topic

    defined, 10–11

    Element 1: access, 11, 16–19, 44

    Element 2: commerce, 11, 20–22, 44

    Element 3: communication, 11, 23–25, 44

    Element 4: literacy, 11, 26–28, 44

    Element 5: etiquette, 11, 29–31, 44

    Element 6: law, 11, 31–34, 44

    Element 7: rights and responsibilities, 11,
35–37, 44

    Element 8: health and wellness, 11, 38–40,
44

    Element 9: security, 11, 40–42, 44

    flexibility, 15–16

    matching activity to recognize, 99–101

    purpose and goals of, 12, 44

    recognizing, classroom foundational
lessons, 99–101

    understanding, 43–44

P

parents

    blog for parent communication, 67–68

    digital citizenship, 138

performance. *See* student academic learning and
performance

personal security. *See* security

phishing, 147

plagiarize, defined, 147

plagiarism guided lesson, 125–126

podcasting, 148

    primer on, 64

practice, reflection model, 84, 85

primer

    on blogs, 62

    on MP3 files and players, 122

    on podcasting, 64

    on Twitter, 66

    on wikis, 68

professional development activities, 55–80
    activity format, 56
    introduction to digital citizenship, 57–59
    outside school environment. *See* student life outside the school environment
    schools, creating digital citizenship programs in, 55–80
    student academic learning and performance activities, 60–70
    student environment and behavior activities, 71–77
protections. *See* security
purchasing items online. *See* commerce

R

race and ethnicity, digital divide, 17–18
ranking, digital vs. nondigital school issues, 76
reflection model, 83–87
    diagram, 84
    stage 1: awareness, 84, 85
    stage 2: guided practice, 84, 85
    stage 3: modeling and demonstration, 84, 86
    stage 4: feedback and analysis, 84, 86–87
resources
    access, 19
    AUP, 13
    blogs, 62
    commerce, 22
    communication, 25
    etiquette, 31
    health and wellness, 40
    law, 34
    literacy, 28
    plagiarism, 125–126
    podcasting, 64
    rights and responsibilities, 37
    security, 42
    Twitter, 66
    wikis, 66
rights and responsibilities
    appropriate technology use activity, 71
    cyberbullying guided lesson, 124–125
    digital citizenship and the district AUP activity, 74–76
    digital rights management (DRM) activity, 78
    inappropriate technology use activity, 72
    nine elements framework, 11, 35–37, 44
    plagiarism guided lesson, 125–126
RSS, for web content syndication, 148
rubric
    classroom, guided lessons in digital citizenship, 134–135
    classroom foundational lessons, 113–114

S

school digital citizenship
    creating programs in, 45–80
        digital citizenship audit and form, 50–51
        lessons learned from other schools/ districts, 53–54
        life outside school. *See* student life outside the school environment
        plan development, 48–50
        plan implementation, 52
        professional development activities, 55–80
        technology leadership team, 47
    student environment and behavior
        Activities, 71–77
        Guided Lessons, 124–128
        in nine elements framework, 44
    student life outside the school environment
        Activities, 78–80
        Guided Lessons, 129–133
        in nine elements framework, 44
scoring rubric
    classroom, guided lessons in digital citizenship, 134–135
    classroom foundational lessons, 113–114
search engine, 148
security
    nine elements framework, 11, 40–42, 44
    protecting personal activity, 77
    protecting the school's network guided lesson, 128
selling items online. *See* commerce
sexting, 32, 148
smartphone, 3, 22, 26, 110, 140, 148
social network, 148
socioeconomic status, digital divide, 17–18
standards
    NETS•A, 3, 56, 90, 159–160
    NETS•S, 3, 90, 155–156
    NETS•T, 3, 56, 90, 157–158
student academic learning and performance
    Activities, 60–70
        appreciation blog, 61–62
        blogs and wikis for parent communication, 67–68
        new digital communication models, 63–64
        providing digital access outside school, 70
        technology use in education, 69
        Twitter for gathering information, 65–66
        understanding digital technologies, 60

Guided Lessons, 117–123
  appropriate Internet use, 119
  bridging the digital divide, 123
  business use of technology, 120
  cell phone interruptions, 117
  message misinterpretation, 118
  MP3 files for teaching, 121–122
in nine elements framework, 44
student environment and behavior
  Activities, 71–77
    appropriate technology use, 71
    digital citizenship and the district
      AUP, 74–76
    digital etiquette issues, 73
    inappropriate technology use, 72
    protecting personal security, 77
  etiquette
    digital issues activity, 73
    netiquette, defined, 147
    nine elements framework, 11, 29–31,
      44
    when working online guided lesson,
      127
  Guided Lessons, 124–128
    cyberbullying, 124–125
    digital etiquette when working online,
      127
    digital plagiarism, 125–126
    protecting the school's network, 128
  in nine elements framework, 44
student life outside the school environment
  Activities, 78–80
    buying items online, 79
    digital rights management, 78
    technology addiction, 80
  Guided Lessons, 129–133
    buying and selling on auction sites,
      130–131
    buying items online, 129–130
    computer ergonomics, 132–133
    file sharing, 133
    free time choices, 131–132
  in nine elements framework, 44
survey, digital *vs.* nondigital school issues, 75
syndication of web content, 148

T

target for digital citizenship, 138
technology
  addiction activity, 80
  creating leadership team, 47
  distance learning, 145
  educational standards for
    NETS•A, 3, 56, 90, 159–160
    NETS•S, 3, 90, 155–156
    NETS•T, 3, 56, 90, 157–158
  integration of, 148
text messaging, 148
3G, 148
Twitter, 65–66, 139, 148
  primer on, 66

U

URL, 148

V

virtual, as term, 149

W

Web 2.0, 149
web browser, 143
web logs. *See* blogs
web resources. *See* resources
wellness. *See* health and wellness
Wi-Fi, 149
Wi-Fi hotspot, 146
wikis
  described, 68, 149
  new digital communication models activity,
    63–64
  for parent communication activity, 67–68
  primer on, 68
wireless, 149
working online, etiquette guided lesson, 127

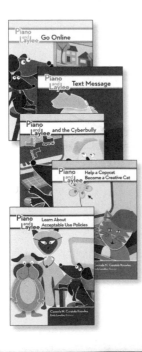